GUTS

—AND—

GLORY

Also by Ken Rappoport,
available from Walker and Company

Grant Hill
Shaquille O'Neal
Bobby Bonilla

GUTS
—— **A N D** ——
GLORY

MAKING IT IN THE NBA

Ken Rappoport

Walker and Company
New York

For Adina

First published in the United States of America in 1997 by Walker Publishing Company, Inc.

Published simultaneously in Canada by Thomas Allen & Son Canada, Limited, Markham, Ontario

Library of Congress Cataloging-in-Publication Data

Rappoport, Ken.
Guts and glory: making it in the NBA/Ken Rappoport.
p. cm.
Includes bibliographical references (p.) and index.
Summary: Examines the lives of ten professional basketball players, including Muggsy Bogues, Bobby Hurley, John Lucas, Hakeem Olajuwon, and Buck Williams, who overcame various obstacles on their way to success in the NBA.
ISBN 0-8027-8430-5 (hc). —ISBN 0-8027-8431-3
1. Basketball players—United States—Biography—Juvenile literature.   2. National Basketball Association—Juvenile literature.   [1. Basketball players.   2. Perseverance (Ethics)]
I. Title.
GV884.A1R355   1997
796.323'64'092273—dc21
[B]   96-48212
CIP   AC

Printed in the United States of America

2   4   6   8   10   9   7   5   3   1

Contents

Preface   vii
Acknowledgments   ix

1. Mahmoud Abdul-Rauf (Chris Jackson)   1
2. Muggsy Bogues   15
3. Bobby Hurley   29
4. John Lucas   41
5. Reggie Miller   53
6. Hakeem Olajuwon   67
7. John Starks   83
8. Isiah Thomas   95
9. Buck Williams   109
10. Hot Rod Williams   123

Source Notes   135
Index   143

Preface

So few would-be Michael Jordans actually fulfill their dreams of making it in the National Basketball Association. Imagine having to overcome a major problem to do so?

This book is about ten special athletes who battled adversity to make their mark in the NBA, the world's best professional basketball league. While their stories are different, they are all linked by a similar theme: courage.

As you will see, courage comes in all shapes and sizes: a player who was big but inexperienced and a player whom many considered too small; a player who was waiting to be discovered and one who had no place to hide.

These stories are about more than basketball. They are about fulfilling dreams and goals, about never giving up although the odds are against you. They also underscore a universal truth: The tougher the road, the sweeter the reward at the end of it.

Acknowledgments

The author wishes to thank the following for their help with this book: Buck Williams, Lefty Driesell, Greg Manning, Reggie Henderson, Jack Zane, Dick Harter, Merianne Snow, Bob Wade, Bob Staak, Ernie Nestor, George Whittaker, Leonard Hamilton, Bill Self, Mike Bree, Walt Hazzard, Dave Rose, Guy Lewis, Johnny Jones, Craig Carse, Bert Jenkins, Gene Pingatore, Jim Garcia, Marty McNeal, Al Biancani, Gary Gerould, Mike Peplowski, Kirk Saulny, Roy Danforth, Tom Green, Larry Nance, Blake Kling, John Gates, Bob Zink, Bettina Wright, and Tom McMillen. Once again, my thanks to Mary Perrotta Rich for initiating another special project for me at Walker and Company. And of course, to my wife, Bernice, for her always invaluable input into my books.

GUTS

—— A N D ——

GLORY

1

MAHMOUD ABDUL-RAUF
(Chris Jackson)

Mahmoud Abdul-Rauf was involved in a painfully difficult task. It was a morning workout, and the Denver Nuggets star guard was trying to lace up his sneakers.

He measured the laces carefully so they were even on each side, then started to thread them through the eyelets.

Too short on one side, Abdul-Rauf decided. Do it again.

He tried a second time. No good.

Then a third. Still didn't feel right. Would he ever get it right? Lines of concentration were etched on his face as he tried again and again.

Finally, after twenty minutes, the laces matched perfectly on both sides. Abdul-Rauf breathed a sigh of relief. What most children could do in a minute or two was an incredibly difficult task for the twenty-five-year-old professional basketball player.

Such painful perfectionism had tormented

Showing drive at LSU. Then he was known as Chris Jackson. *(LSU)*

Abdul-Rauf since childhood. He has Tourette's syndrome, a neurological disorder of the brain.

"There are some days I get to practice and I'm beat," he said. "I'm fighting myself all morning. Getting dressed, I'm tucking in my shirt for ten minutes. I have to. If I don't, I'll feel crooked out there. Tying my shoes, and touching everything. People just don't know."[1]

It is not the only symptom of Tourette's. Abdul-Rauf cannot go through a day without some sign of his quirky disorder. He can make all kinds of weird faces that could make you laugh, but he isn't having any fun. Repetitive grimaces and tics can overwhelm his body. And then there are the unexpected sounds. He can be alone or in a crowd and he suddenly lets out a loud whoop, or a grunt. People stare. Sometimes it's a snort, or he might actually bark, and he can't stop himself. It is all involuntary.

The illness is a mystery, as mysterious today as when it was first described by French neurologist Gilles de la Tourette in 1885.

Some 200,000 Americans suffer from Tourette's, but they are not on display in front of the public playing in the high-pressure world of the NBA. Abdul-Rauf has managed to survive and thrive in this climate despite his disorder.

He was born Chris Jackson in Gulfport, Mississippi, a town of beaches and basketball courts near the Gulf of Mexico. When his mother gave him a toy basketball as a toddler, he carried it with him wherever he went. It was symbolic.

There would be very few moments in his life when he wouldn't have a basketball with him. The courts were within walking distance of his home, and there weren't many days he missed using them. In his first game with his fourth-grade team, he scored 21 points. When he heard the crowd cheering, he was hooked.

Chris loved Julius Erving, the sky-walking Hall of Fame forward. He couldn't wait to get on the court and try to duplicate Dr. J's moves. In summers, he played from early morning until late into the night. In winters, he woke before dawn to practice before he went to school. When he came home, he practiced again.

Only it wasn't the way ordinary people practiced. It wasn't just making the shots, it was how the ball swished through the net. All the shots had to be perfect, had to feel "just right." He didn't understand why he did what he did. But oddly, Tourette's played a role in his development as a basketball player.

"Every day, before I got off the court, there was this routine I had to finish," Jackson said. "I couldn't miss a shot. If I missed on the last shot, I'd have to start over.

"In that routine, I'd go full speed. I can remember missing the last shot and having to start over and over again. I'd be breathing hard and sweating, and I couldn't catch my breath; I'd be gasping for air, burning up, thinking, *Man, I'm going to have heat stroke*. But I kept doing it."[2]

He built up his body. He ran backward on the beach wearing combat boots. He held weights in his hand and did toe raises. He jumped up and down off a three-foot porch, "anything I could think of, everything I could do to try to get better."³

Gulfport High School coach Bert Jenkins saw him as a sixth-grader and thought: *What a prospect!* He couldn't wait to coach him. And when he arrived, Chris Jackson's quest for perfection disrupted practice sessions. Unintentionally, of course.

Coach Jenkins liked to begin every practice session by having his players shoot twenty free throws. Make all twenty, then shoot until you miss. Chris Jackson would make his twenty and keep on shooting. And shooting.

"One day he just couldn't miss. He hit 283 straight," Jenkins remembered. "The guy who was throwing them back to him was utterly exhausted. To show it wasn't an accident, about a week later he hit 267 straight, another time 243. He shot for forty-five minutes. We didn't have much time for practice."⁴

Jackson's condition made him seek perfection not only in basketball, but also in everyday routine tasks.

One day, Coach Jenkins noticed a long line at the water fountain in the gym. Chris Jackson was standing at the front.

"He would reach for the handle and turn the water on and then draw it back, and reach again, over and over," Jenkins remembered.⁵

As far back as Chris Jackson could remember, he had this mysterious ailment. *There goes the*

Jackson boy—strange, isn't he? That's what the neighbors would think as they watched young Jackson twitch uncontrollably, emit weird sounds for no apparent reason, or buckle and rebuckle his seat belt in a car countless number of times. In junior high school, the condition worsened. He would stand in front of a mirror and watch his shoulders jerk, his eyes blink wildly.

"God, help me stop!"[6]

He cried himself to sleep, wondering what was wrong, wondering if he would die. There were the blackouts during the day—too many of them. It was frightening.

"Someone would have to touch me or scream at me to get my attention," he said. "It was scary, because I didn't know when I would black out again."[7]

Doctors wrongfully diagnosed Chris as an epileptic. They gave him pills. But the pills made him sick, and he would sometimes pretend to take them, then hide them in the brick walls at home.

The symptoms continued, particularly his obsession for perfection.

Reading became a challenge. "Each sentence has to come from my mind exactly right, and then it has to come off my lips right when I say it out loud, and then I have to get the meaning right. When I was a kid trying to study, I'd spend an hour sometimes getting just one sentence perfect."[8]

Was it something he had inherited from his mother? Jacqueline Jackson, while raising three boys alone, was obsessive to an abnormal degree. She would drive halfway to work, only to return home to check if she had locked the front door or turned off the lights.

Lil Jenkins, the coach's wife, wanted to solve the mystery. A former nurse, she was concerned about the seventeen-year-old Jackson. Upset about the misery he was in, and suspecting Tourette's, she persuaded him to see a neurologist. The doctor confirmed her suspicion.

"When I found out there was a name for what I had, I felt a lot better," Jackson said. "I knew I wasn't the only one in the world, and there was something I could do for it."[9]

He was given medication to help control the disorder, although sometimes it left him sluggish. Yet he still had enough spark to lead his team to two state championships and win Mississippi Player of the Year two times.

It was scholarship time. And a big battle was brewing, not only among the colleges but on the home front. Chris was sold on Louisiana State University and Dale Brown's system of play. He would be starting as a freshman and would have the freedom to be creative. He signed a letter of intent to join the Tigers. His mother ripped it up. She wanted him to look at other schools. Against his mother's wishes, he showed up on the LSU campus to start his freshman year. And what a freshman year it was.

In just his third game at LSU, Jackson scored

48 points. Amazing. Freshmen aren't expected to produce such startling numbers. What he did next was even better.

A few days later, Jackson played his first road game when LSU traveled to Florida to play the University of Florida, one of the nation's top-ranked teams. As Jackson walked out of his hotel with LSU assistant coach Craig Carse, he was worried.

"How good is this team? What can we do?" Jackson asked Carse.

"Well, if you get forty points, we have a chance," Carse answered.

Early in the game, one of the Florida players slapped Jackson on the back of the head to try to intimidate him. It backfired. "When they poked Chris in the head, I knew right then—they're done!" Carse remembered. "He's so competitive that if you try to intimidate him or push him around, you don't have a chance."[10]

Jackson scored 53 points, an NCAA record for a freshman, and LSU beat the heavily favored Gators, 111–101.

Jackson had a spectacular first year, with a 30.2 scoring average, a record for a freshman. He became only the second player in college history to be named to the Associated Press All-America first team as a freshman. When he virtually repeated his performance as a sophomore, Jackson had established some mind-boggling stats: He scored in double figures in 63 of the 64 games he had played.

On the rare nights he was off his game, he went back to the drawing board—or, in his case, the gym. One morning after missing 14 of 23 shots against Kentucky, Jackson woke up the student manager so he could get on the court and practice. Jackson didn't stop shooting "until I got it right."[11]

Tourette's could not diminish Jackson's brilliance, even though it caused distractions at times, on and off the court.

When the game was fast-paced and exciting, and everyone was running downcourt, all of a sudden Jackson would erupt in loud "Whoops" and "Ba-BOOMS." The unexpected shouts startled everyone on the court. In the NBA, officials interpreted Jackson's facial expressions as criticism of their rulings and slapped him with technicals. In college, Coach Brown constantly found himself defending and explaining Jackson's involuntary actions to the officials. In the locker room, no one was safe standing next to Jackson. They could end up with black-and-blue bruises. Without warning, Jackson would suddenly swing out with an involuntary slash of his arm. His locker-room neighbors learned to be wary.

When interviewed, particularly for television, Jackson fought the enemy within and maintained composure as best he could. Then, when the interview was over, he would head straight for a room, slam the door, and let out all his pent-up emotions.

"There were times when he was ready to explode," Brown said. "When he twitched and barked, his teammates had to hold his hands and put their arms around him."[12]

Jackson was one of the most popular athletes ever at LSU. Fans, young and old, flocked to him. He was a perfect role model for children, because they could more easily relate to the 5-foot-11, 140-pound Jackson than to 300-pound seven-footers. The good-natured Jackson never refused an autograph or a request for his time.

After a loss at Alabama, Coach Brown was approached by a woman. Her daughter had Tourette's and wanted to meet Jackson. No problem.

Brown, the woman, and the girl went to the hotel, where the team had just sat down for the postgame meal. Jackson was about to dig into his steak when he was called away. One hour later, he was still talking to the young girl. He never finished his steak.

"We'd get bags of mail from kids who had Tourette's and had been inspired after listening to him talk," Brown said. "This is a person who came out of poverty. He lived at the end of a dirt road in a shack with no father in the home."[13]

On a visit home, Jackson finally made The Decision. He opened the refrigerator to find only eggs and water. When the kitchen sink came loose from the plaster wall and crashed to the floor, that's when he decided to leave college for the pros. "She couldn't live like that anymore," he said, referring to his mom. "That's when I resolved to get the money so that she wouldn't have to."[14]

With his extraordinary accomplishments at LSU, he knew he would be a high draft pick by an NBA team.That meant big money, enough to give him and his family security for the rest of their lives.

The Denver Nuggets drafted Jackson even though they were concerned about his neurological condition. When he reported to camp, he gave them another reason for concern. Told he needed to bulk up for the pros, he had put on too much weight. He was sluggish. He wasn't able to keep up with the Nuggets' high-tempo running game under Coach Paul Westhead.

That wasn't his only problem. Born with an extra bone near both his ankles that caused him considerable pain, Jackson needed surgery. He decided to wait until the end of the season. He suffered through his rookie year, missing 14 games.

Jackson's relationship with Westhead became strained. He lost playing time and confidence. After his first NBA season, Jackson said: "I was mad and frustrated."[15]

His second season was worse. Jackson was getting less playing time. "If Chris came in the game and missed his first two or three shots, he wasn't going to play the rest of the night," remembered

Mahmoud Abdul-Rauf: Always seeking perfection.
(Denver Nuggets)

Dan Issel, a former player who was the television colorman for the Nuggets games.[16]

That changed when Issel replaced Westhead as coach. "I had seen him in college and I knew what kind of player he was," Issel said. "I didn't know what had transpired between him and Paul, but this would be a new start."[17]

The new start featured not only a new coach but a new religion. During his trying times with Westhead, Jackson embraced the Islamic religion, eventually changing his name to Mahmoud (pronounced "MOCK-mood") Abdul-Rauf. The religion helped him accept his condition. He believed that Tourette's was an affliction he had to bear. He had come to terms with it.

Guided by Islam, he worked hard during the summer. Dawn to dusk. Just like the old days. He reported to training camp for the 1992–93 season in the best physical condition of his career. His stats for the season showed it. Jackson boosted his scoring average to such a degree that he was named the NBA's Most Improved Player. In the 1993–94 season, he missed only 10 foul shots. His .956 percentage was the second best in NBA history.

The Tourette's syndrome was still with him, but he succeeded in spite of it.

"When I'm on the court I notice that I'm having tics—but I really don't notice it as something that bothers my game," said Abdul-Rauf, who now plays for the Sacramento Kings.[18]

Islam had given him something more than a

name. It gave him a purpose and a sense of inner peace. It was actually the ideal religion for him. Islam stresses the quest for perfection. And who better than Mahmoud Abdul-Rauf to seek perfection?

2

MUGGSY BOGUES

It was the high school game of the year. The Dunbar Poets faced the Camden Panthers in a battle of unbeaten powers. Another big test for Dunbar. A bigger one for Muggsy Bogues.

He waited anxiously on the sidelines as the announcer's voice blared over the loudspeaker. The gym exploded with cheers as the home team was introduced.

Then it was Dunbar's turn.

As he trotted onto the court, Muggsy got a tremendous response from the crowd. But it wasn't applause. People were standing and pointing. They were doubling up with laughter.

"That little kid . . . that little guy is going to play against us?" echoed throughout the Camden gym.[1] Muggsy, just over five feet tall, was the object of their taunts.

Dunbar coach Bob Wade gathered his players around him before the game started and turned to Muggsy.

"Short man, are you okay?"[2]

Bogues looked straight at Wade. He shrugged it off. He was just fine. In fact, Bogues promised, he

---

Running the show at Charlotte. *(Charlotte Hornets)*

would have the last laugh when the game was over.

Muggsy always had his doubters, from the age of seven when he started playing basketball. In high school. In college. In the NBA.

At 5 feet 3, he is the shortest player in NBA history.

Bogues's family would never be confused with Andre the Giant's. His father was 5 feet 6, his mother 4 feet 11. Muggsy was in between, but still shorter than his two older brothers. He was thrilled when he broke the five-foot barrier in high school.

Born Tyrone Bogues in Baltimore, he began playing organized ball in the recreational leagues. He won an unusual nickname for the fierce way he played defense. Neighborhood kids said he seemed to be "mugging" people on the court. "Mugger" soon became "Muggsy."

The games were played in the tough Lafayette section of Baltimore, where life was hard and sometimes cheap. You had to be lucky just to get out alive. The projects had it all, and not much of it was good: crime and drugs, muggings and murder.

Bogues grew up with gunshots ringing in his ears. The 'Hood was like a war zone. One of the casualties of the war was Skip Wise. He was a talented basketball player, a star at Clemson who eventually flunked out. When his pro career turned sour, Skip turned back to the streets and got caught up in drugs. He wound up in jail. The prospect of turning out like Skip scared Muggsy. He resolved not to follow in Skip's footsteps.

Muggsy's father, Richard, was another casualty. He was sent to prison for armed robbery and drug dealing. The thought of his father in jail haunted Muggsy, so he stayed away from gangs and drugs. His mother, the strongest influence in his life, provided support and a positive example by going for her high school diploma while raising the family. It was a time for celebration when she went off welfare and went to work.

In his neighborhood, Muggsy needed all the family support he could get. "All it would take was about two seconds to get into trouble or get killed," he said.[3]

The only shooting Muggsy wanted to do was with a basketball. He was never without one. "I'd even dribble a basketball when I'd throw out the trash—and I got so that I could do it without spilling the trash."[4]

But nobody figured him for a basketball player at his height. He was always the last chosen in playground games. One day Muggsy came home crying. He wanted to be tall. "You'll do fine," his mother, Elaine Bogues, said as she hugged him. "God doesn't make mistakes."[5]

And Muggsy made very few on the court. He was a totally unselfish player. He didn't need to score all the points himself. He liked to get his teammates involved in the game. Everyone loved playing with him.

Coach Wade noticed Muggsy for the first time

when he came to the Dunbar gym to play in pickup games after the varsity had finished practice. He was impressed. "He could really hold his own against the taller and older kids."[6]

Still, Wade was skeptical that Muggsy could play varsity ball at his height—shorter than his brother Anthony, who had been a starting point guard at Dunbar.

Sure, Muggsy could stand tall in recreation-league competition, but what about the next level? Surely, his lack of height would be a serious deficit in high school.

But his brother had done it. Anything Anthony could do, Muggsy was determined to do.

"When someone tells him he can't do something, he works that much harder," said his mother.[7]

Muggsy desperately wanted to go to Dunbar, the school with the BIG basketball reputation. All his friends were going there. He applied to Dunbar—or thought he had. There was a mix-up. His transcript was sent to the wrong school. The unhappy Muggsy was going to Southern High School many miles away—even though Dunbar was right across the street. Muggsy had to wait to transfer.

As a junior, he joined a powerhouse Dunbar team that included childhood friends David Wingate and Reggie Williams, along with Reggie Lewis, all of whom would go on to play professional basketball.

Muggsy now had to make a believer of Wade. Muggsy believed, regardless of his size, that he could get the job done. He wasn't going to listen to the critics. He was going to prove them wrong. He passed his first big test, winning Most Valuable Player in the prestigious Harlem City Tournament in New York.

Later in the season, the Poets were still unbeaten after 24 games. But they had yet to face Camden High School. The New Jersey school was ranked No. 1 in the country.

Walking into Camden High's noisy, raucous gym was enough to throw any team off its stride. The powerful Panthers were virtually unbeatable there. "You'd always try to play them at a neutral site," Wade said.[8] Would this be the end of Dunbar's winning streak?

When Muggsy lined up against Camden star Kevin Walls for the start of the game, he looked like someone's kid brother who had accidentally wandered onto the court. The crowd roared with laughter. The Camden guard, who was several inches taller, laughed and brushed him aside with a wave of his hand. *He's nothing—I can handle this kid.*

The joke, as it turned out, was on Camden High.

Muggsy had his best game: 15 points, 12 assists, 6 steals. He made sure Walls had one of his worst, stealing the ball from him 7 times and holding him to under 10 points.

Final: Dunbar 84, Camden 59. The Poets finished the season undefeated and ranked No. 1 in the country—a performance they would repeat the following year.

Suddenly, the "short man" had developed a tall profile. He was voted the Most Valuable Player on one of the most powerful high school teams in history. Now he was being watched. Ernie Nestor, an assistant coach at Wake Forest, had kept an eye on Muggsy in summer camps and in his senior year. Two things especially stood out: his pressure defense and his ability to move the ball upcourt. "He could put the ball at the top of the key with the clock at twenty-one," Nestor said. "That's a great advantage for a team."[9] Teams had to shoot the ball within 24 seconds or lose possession. Muggsy needed only three seconds or so to get the ball into shooting position.

Once Wake Forest offered a scholarship, Muggsy didn't need much time to make his decision. There weren't that many offers. Now he would be going to a classy major-school program in the Atlantic Coast Conference, one of the best basketball leagues in the country.

First, Wade extracted a promise from Demon Deacons coach Carl Tacy that Muggsy would have a chance to play regularly. "I wanted to make sure he was not going to be used as a sideshow," Wade said.[10]

In his first year at Wake Forest, Muggsy played in the shadow of starting point guard Danny Young and averaged only 10 minutes a game.

While he was overshadowed on the basketball court, he was overwhelmed in the classroom. Muggsy had a tough time making the adjustment to a college environment. He was discouraged. It was a time of soul-searching. He thought about

Muggsy Bogues made a sizable contribution to Wake Forest basketball. *(Wake Forest)*

leaving Wake Forest, but realized he would probably find the same situation at other schools. Besides, Muggsy never considered himself a quitter. He decided to stick it out.

The second year at Wake Forest was better. Young had graduated, and Muggsy was handed the starting point guard position.

Halfway through the season, he faced the biggest test of his young college career when the Demon Deacons met a powerful Duke team at the Blue Devils' arena. The Blue Devils were ranked No. 2 in the country and featured Johnny Dawkins, the top-scoring guard in the ACC. Dawkins had scored in double figures in 51 straight games.

Muggsy's assignment: Shut down Dawkins.

That wasn't his only problem. Muggsy was about to be shot down himself—literally. He had received a death threat and everyone was taking it seriously. Someone had threatened to shoot Muggsy if he stepped on the court against Duke.

The FBI was brought in as Muggsy learned about the threat. He just shrugged his shoulders. He had faced worse in his own neighborhood, hadn't he?

Death threats and Duke fans—a lethal combination. Law-enforcement officials were standing behind the Wake Forest bench. When Muggsy came out on the court, the Duke fans started chanting, "Stand up, stand up!"

Ignoring the pressure and the taunts, all Muggsy did was play one of the greatest games of his college career. He held Dawkins to 8 points and

Muggsy Bogues earned his nickname for his fierce defense.
(Wake Forest)

scored 12 himself, along with 7 assists and 4 steals. The game was still up for grabs, though, with nine seconds left when Muggsy went to the foul line in a one-on-one situation. More pressure. He had to make the first shot in order to get the opportunity to make the second.

He made the first shot, then another.

Wake Forest won, 91–89.

Muggsy was helping to win games, but he still wasn't winning much national attention. That was about to change. Two weeks later, he was on national television in a big ACC game against North Carolina State. You knew it was big because well-known basketball analyst Al McGuire was there. McGuire had coached Marquette to the national championship and had seen it all. He wasn't easily impressed.

Muggsy faced another of the country's top guards, Spud Webb of North Carolina State. If Muggsy was going to show his stuff, this was a good time.

He went to work: 20 points, 10 assists, 4 steals. Now McGuire was impressed.

"I've never seen a player dominate a game the way he did,"[11] McGuire raved following Wake Forest's 91–64 victory over the Wolfpack.

Muggsy was a national sensation. And now he was about to spark an international explosion.

It was an exciting time for Muggsy that summer. He was in Spain with the U.S. team to play in the World Basketball Championships. The sight of the tiny American challenging and blowing away the taller competition created a sensation. Children, enchanted by his tiny size, flocked to him. Muggsy turned anti-American crowds into red, white, and blue supporters, as they clapped furiously every time he touched the ball. Round after round, Muggsy was the U.S. ambassador of goodwill as he led the Americans to the gold medal. Reporters nicknamed him "La Crispa Negra" ("The Black Spark") for his dynamic play. "He appears to be a little brother of his teammates," wrote one reporter, "but it is he who orders, commands, and directs."[12]

He was so popular that he was invited to be the grand marshal at a local celebration, but NCAA rules prohibited the trip.

They appreciated him at the World Basketball Championships. Would Muggsy be appreciated in the NBA?

Once again Muggsy found skeptics following his announcement of his intention to play in the pros. "All I ask for is a chance," Muggsy said. "It's just a matter of who wants to take that chance."[13]

Mel Daniels, the assistant general manager of the Indiana Pacers, didn't. "I don't think he'd get a shot off in the pros, and defensively he can't stop anybody."[14]

But Muggsy had no intention of giving up. "All my life, people have been telling me I'm too small to compete on the next level. But basketball isn't for big people, it's for people who can play the game."[15]

The washington Bullets took a chance on Muggsy, but then they didn't give him a chance. He saw limited action. Muggsy was literally playing in a land of giants. Every player that Muggsy faced was taller. Some of the matchups looked comical—the tiny figure of Muggsy barely above the waistlines of many of his towering opponents. Bogues was nearly a foot and a half shorter than the average NBA player. For the first time in his career, Muggsy doubted himself. He was down and wasn't sure he was going to make it. His friend and teammate, Moses Malone, lifted his spirits.

"Don't worry, you'll get your chance—you'll make it."[16]

A new expansion team, the Charlotte Hornets, was looking for talent. The Bullets let him go in the expansion draft. Surely, with an expansion team Muggsy would get more playing time. But all he did was come off the bench as a replacement—Coach Dick Harter didn't think he was tall enough to be a starter, even though Muggsy made an impact when he was in the game.

Muggsy was puzzled. "I never could understand this, because every time I was in the game, the team picked up. If I could do it for short spurts, why not give me a chance to do it for longer spurts?"[17] Muggsy knew he had to keep going.

"I had a coach who didn't believe in me. So I had to keep believing, keep staying focused, and that's what I was able to do. I didn't let anything get me off track."[18]

Muggsy finally got his chance. When Allan Bristow became the Hornets' coach, Muggsy was starting and running the show in Charlotte. Muggsy has since been named the Hornets' Most

Valuable Player twice. He has been an MVP at every level he has played!

As a pro, Muggsy has continually defied the odds, even in the face of great personal tragedy. Before the 1993–94 season, he lost two of the most important people in his life—his father and his best friend, Reggie Lewis.

Lewis was a star for the Boston Celtics. So when he collapsed and died of a heart attack while shooting baskets, it made national headlines. It became a double tragedy for Muggsy when his father, who had had health problems since his release from prison, died three days after Lewis's funeral. And when it looked as if nothing more could happen, there was another death on the same day—the uncle of Muggsy's wife. Through it all, however, he managed to have his best season.

"I just realize that life goes on," Muggsy said. "I spoke to those guys [his father and Lewis] in my prayers, and I found that inner strength from them. Letting them know I'm all right, things are okay."[19]

Bogues calls himself a "living example of not giving up."[20] There aren't any doubters now.

3

BOBBY HURLEY

It wasn't just another NBA season-opening game for Bobby Hurley. He was more nervous than he could ever remember as he tucked his shirt into the shorts of his crisp white Sacramento Kings uniform. The basketball court at the ARCO Arena wasn't more than a few steps away. But for Hurley, it was the longest walk he had ever taken in his life.

Too many questions flooded his mind as he took the court for warm-ups. The biggest one: *Can I make it back?*

That was the question in the minds of many others as they watched Hurley warm up. The horrifying specter of the auto accident was still fresh.

Less than a year earlier, on the evening of December 12, 1993, Hurley was driving his sport utility truck home after a game when it happened. He was making a left turn at a stop sign about a mile from the arena when he was struck by a station wagon. The impact hurled his truck some one hundred feet. Hurley was thrown forty feet, into a drainage canal.

Duke basketball was in good hands with Bobby Hurley.
(Duke University)

Mike Peplowski, one of Hurley's teammates, was among the first to arrive on the scene. The fellow rookie had left the arena shortly after Hurley had. He wrapped Hurley in a hunting jacket that he had in his truck, then helped carry him out of the ditch.

"Am I going to die?" Hurley asked Peplowski.[1]

On the East Coast, Hurley's parents had watched their son's frustrating game earlier that evening on the satellite dish. Hurley had played only 19 minutes and was held scoreless in a 112–102 loss to the Los Angeles Clippers. Bob and Chris Hurley had gone to bed in their modest brick row home in Jersey City, New Jersey, only to be awakened after midnight by the phone.

It was Richard Marder, the Sacramento Kings' team doctor.

"Bobby has been in a serious accident," he said. "He will be undergoing emergency surgery, and we're fairly certain he will survive. I need you to get on a plane right away."[2]

Bob Hurley paled. The words "fairly certain" suddenly took on a new meaning in his life. But he knew his son was a battler. He had shown his competitive spirit and courage in many ways on a basketball court.

Bobby Hurley had been toughened on the basketball playgrounds of Jersey City. His father, Bob Hurley Sr., was the basketball coach at St. Anthony High School, which had one of the top Catholic basketball programs in America. He had the championship rings to prove it.

Bob Hurley, who also worked as a probation officer, was tough on his players. That went double for Bobby, even before he played for his father at St. Anthony. There were brutal one-on-one games between father and son, played for more than just family pride. The same later held true for Bobby's younger brother, Danny. "I've been very tough on the boys," Bob Hurley later said. "But I tried to keep them out of trouble and build up their competitiveness."[3]

The Hurley family credo: Nothing worthwhile comes easy.

"He pushed hard," Danny said, "but there are boundaries, and my dad never crossed them."[4]

But Bobby eventually crossed town to face the tough competition in the "projects" where the best basketball in Jersey City was being played.

It was a challenge.

"If I had stayed in my own neighborhood, nothing would have happened,"[5] said Hurley, who was small and frail-looking compared to the big, broad-shouldered athletes he faced.

But even though he was in the minority as a small, white guard, he never felt out of place. His friends were there, and so was the fiercest competition.

Certainly, few players had grown up with more of a love for basketball. Having the high school coach at home helped. Young Bobby had more insights, was more mentally prepared to play the game, than most. He had no choice. He wasn't a physical presence like many of the athletes he faced.

"When he was in the seventh grade and about four feet, ten inches tall, he was able to handle himself in fast-break drills with my high school team," Bob Hurley remembered. "As a freshman for me at St. Anthony, he still looked like a midget with the ball. But even then, he could influence the game."[6]

Frail-looking. Too small. Not a great shooter. That's what they said about Bobby Hurley. But looks could be deceiving. "Winner" would be a more likely description: four straight state parochial championships at St. Anthony, including a 32–0 record and the No. 1 ranking in the country in his senior year.

Hurley was a classic point guard who looked to pass before he looked to shoot. His forte was finding the open man. The point guard handles the ball more than anyone on the court. He brings the ball upcourt and sets up plays, sort of like a coach on the floor, and usually determines the flow of a game.

One minute he was the star of a high school team, the next a star at Duke. College freshmen don't usually start. But guess what? Coach Mike Krzyzewski handed Bobby the ball on opening day. Hurley was suddenly running a team in a highly renowned program.

It was a huge responsibility. By the end of the season, the Blue Devils found themselves in the NCAA championship game—pointed there by their determined little point guard who had set Duke's single-season assist record.

Hurley was used to winning championships. But he would not this time. The Blue Devils were given a terrible beating by UNLV in a nationally televised game. Hurley was embarrassed by his performance: two points and five turnovers. He would have given anything to redeem himself. The next year, he had that chance.

Back in the Final Four for the second straight year, the Blue Devils faced the same UNLV team that had run them off the court in 1990. The loss to UNLV had been the lowest point of Hurley's career. The specter of the game had haunted him for a year. Hurley had always been a winner. Could he meet the challenge?

He did. He led the Blue Devils to a 79–77 upset. Hurley played every minute of the 40-minute game, which he called "the closest we've come to being perfect."[7]

The Blue Devils went on to win their first national championship. With Hurley again playing a key role, they repeated in 1992. Six championships in seven years. Not bad for a spunky, frail-looking kid who looked as if he still belonged in the youth leagues of Jersey City.

Next stop: the Sacramento Kings.

The Kings, with one of the NBA's worst all-time winning percentages, expected a great deal from Hurley after signing Duke's golden boy to a six-year, $16.2 million contract. And Hurley expected a lot from himself. But he got off to a slow start. And in the second month of the season, he was still struggling.

It was the Kings' eighteenth game, and Hurley had another bad night. He had seemed out of sync in a loss to the Los Angeles Clippers.

He was taking it hard. He was frustrated and upset with himself when he climbed into his Toyota pickup truck and headed home. The night was unusually cold and damp for California. Hurley's apartment was only a few miles away. His mind may have been a million miles away—he had neglected to put on a seat belt. He stopped at the intersection, still within sight of the arena.

Hurley started to make a left turn. He didn't see the oncoming station wagon on his left and didn't remember the collision that sent him flying through the air. He landed in a drainage ditch, in a life-threatening position: He was facedown in eighteen inches of icy water.

Luck was on Hurley's side. Mike Batham, a passing motorist, stopped. "My first thought," said Batham, "was that he was going to drown if I didn't do something."[8]

Then Peplowski, Hurley's rookie teammate, arrived at the scene. The two men struggled to pull Hurley out of the ditch. "I was more scared than anything. I thought he was going to die," Peplowski confessed.[9]

Could they summon help in time? Luckily, one of the cars had a phone. An ambulance helicopter was immediately summoned. "There was nothing but ambulances and tow trucks and police cars all over the place," remembered Marty McNeal, a beat writer for the *Sacramento Bee*.[10]

Hurley was airlifted to a top-notch trauma center nearby.

Things looked bad at the University of California–Davis Medical Center. Hurley had suffered numerous injuries: two collapsed lungs, five broken ribs, a fractured shoulder blade, torn ligaments in his right knee, a fracture of the lower back, a broken right fibula, a badly sprained wrist, and dozens of deep lacerations and bruises. But the worst of all was a windpipe that had been torn free from one of his lungs.

This injury usually goes undetected in emergency-room treatment and can be fatal. Fortunately for Hurley, the doctor who treated him in the emergency room was an expert on the subject of tracheal and bronchial injury. Dr. Russell Sawyer had recently finished writing a chapter on the subject for a book.

Another stroke of luck: Dr. William Blaisdell, an expert in trauma surgery, was flying in from Washington, D.C., at the moment of the crash. "As we're landing at the airport, my wife looked down at the ground and saw the accident," Blaisdell said.[11] He rushed to the hospital to coordinate Hurley's operation. Hurley underwent eight hours of surgery.

"I don't know of any other patients who have survived this injury," Blaisdell said.[12]

Hurley's parents arrived at the hospital later that day. They hardly recognized their son. Hardened reporters were shocked by what they saw. Gary Gerould, the Kings' play-by-play broadcaster on TV and radio, had done work with motor sports. He had seen race drivers who had taken tremendous beatings and suffered life-threatening injuries. But Gerould was not prepared for what he saw when he first walked into Hurley's hospital room. "It took my breath away. He was absolutely pale, fragile, just broken, like a limp doll."

Yet when Gerould talked to Hurley, he felt a "sense of resolve, of competitiveness, that was already beginning to surface."[13]

It was still touch and go, though. Hurley was learning how to function again. He would try to open his swollen eyes, learn to rise and sit, learn to walk again. To those who thought it was a miracle that Hurley would survive, including the doctors, he had a surprise for everyone: He was out of the hospital in two weeks.

Then the biggest challenge of his life began.

"I had to deal with frustration and depression, the whole mental part of the recovery," Hurley said.[14]

Hurley's main worry was his left shoulder, which had no movement and no strength. He was not able to lift his left arm. He received electrical stimulation and began lifting weights. "Having to go to therapy every day got to be very depressing. There were times when I wouldn't show up. There were times when I wanted to cry because I was so unhappy about what was going on."[15]

Dr. Blaisdell probably would have bet against Hurley playing basketball again, certainly as soon as the following summer. But barely six months later, there he was in the Jersey Shore Summer League.

Hurley's mental condition needed to be shaped up. The games in the summer league had made Hurley both happy and sad. He was thrilled he could be playing competitive basketball so soon after the horrifying accident, but unhappy he couldn't do the things he could do before. He still had his basketball instincts, but his mind was far ahead of his body.

Some days were great, others discouraging. Hurley talked to a sports psychologist, but even that didn't help him stop thinking about quitting the game. One day after a poor performance, Hurley told his father he was finished with basketball.

"It's okay with me if you quit," Bob Hurley told his son, "but first come down to the gym and let's test you. We need to find out if you're just rusty."[16]

Bobby was hesitant when he walked into the gym the next day. His shoulder ached, and so, it seemed, did every bone in his body.

His father began the drills, the same repetitive drills he had known since boyhood: Shoot, pass, dribble. Shoot, pass, dribble. Then start all over again.

Soon his shots were falling through the net. He realized he could play again in the NBA.

That fall, Hurley was back in the Kings' training camp. He had fallen off a mountain, only to climb back up. Not that he was actually at the top just yet.

Hurley's comeback was called a miracle. *(Sacramento Kings)*

Hurley had worked with a physical therapist in the East, then reported to the Kings' strength and conditioning coach, Al Biancani, for more work.

"What I did with him is basically just try to work on restrengthening his total body," Biancani said. "We worked on his range of motion and slowly worked on his cardiovascular, because we had to be very careful with that. Then we worked on flexibility, the total fitness thing."[17]

On the night of November 4, 1994, Bobby Hurley walked nervously onto the court at the ARCO Arena to rousing cheers as he took warm-ups for the opening-night game against the Phoenix Suns. It was his first regular-season game there since the accident.

"It gave me chills," McNeal said, "because just a couple of months before, you wondered if the guy was going to live."[18]

Hurley's return was memorable. His ears were ringing with the cheers of thousands. It was a giant love-in. A huge get-well card with the inscription "We Love You Bobby" flashed in the stands. They loved him more after he led the Kings to a 107–89 victory over the Suns.

A miracle had taken place. Hurley had survived a near-death experience. He wasn't just walking around. He was back playing in the NBA against the finest, quickest, best-conditioned athletes in the world. It was an amazing comeback, a fairy-tale ending.

Dedication and hard work, principles taught to him by his father, had brought him back.

Bobby Hurley was a winner again.

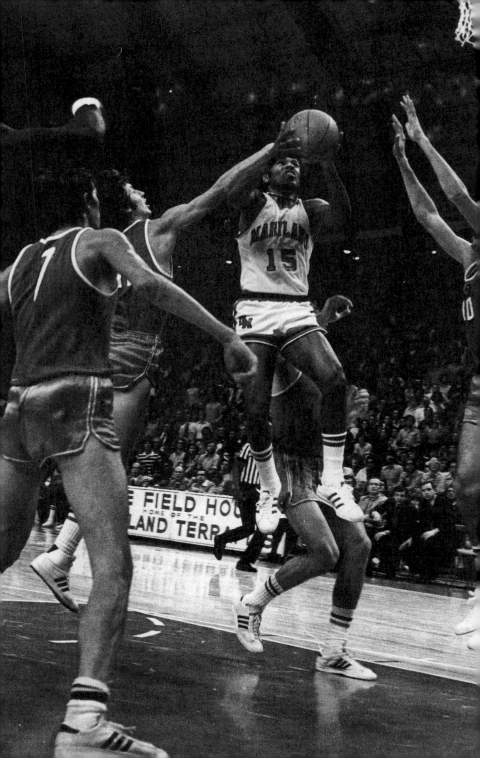

4

JOHN LUCAS

It was a top-secret mission.

John Lucas, former NBA star and drug addict, had arrived one hour before the San Antonio Spurs' game with the Dallas Mavericks and was whisked off to a hiding place in the arena.

Team owner Red McCombs still wasn't sure whether he had made the right decision. He had followed a gut feeling and now, following the game, the Spurs were about to pull off the biggest surprise of the NBA season.

Lucas and McCombs stood in front of the team in the locker room.

"Gentlemen . . . meet the new coach of the Spurs."[1]

The immediate reaction in the dressing room and around the league was shock. John Lucas didn't have any NBA coaching experience. He was a recovering drug addict. He had been suspended twice for cocaine use and kicked off three teams during his often brilliant but troubled fourteen-year NBA career.

The NBA, which had worked hard to clean up

John Lucas: "Trying to be perfect on the basketball court." *(University of Maryland)* its image, didn't quite know what to make of it. Neither did the Spurs players. Lucas was joining a rather eccentric team, one with its own history of confused, tormented souls. That started at the top with McCombs, a recovering alcoholic.

McCombs felt he had nothing to lose in hiring Lucas. The Spurs had already had too many dreary seasons and were going nowhere under Jerry Tarkanian.

In his own words, Lucas had "come back from the dead."[2] Very few had plunged to such depths and survived.

Born in Durham, North Carolina, Lucas had a great start in life. He had all the comforts and loving direction a mom and dad could give. From an early age, he was a competitor, whether in school, sports, or social life.

He had no choice but to do well in school: His mom was his junior high school principal. When he got to high school, there was no relief: His father was the principal there. John idolized him. John Lucas Sr. had been one of the first desegregation leaders in the South. "He became God in my life, and I wanted to be just like him," Lucas said.[3]

John Jr. was cocky. He was the seventh-grader with the ninth-grade girl—nothing was beyond his reach. The driven Lucas set high goals: the first black coach in the NBA, the first black president of the United States. He was valedictorian of his senior class at Hillside High School, but more widely known for his sports accomplishments.

Lucas was a two-sport star. In basketball, he

broke the North Carolina high school career scoring record of the legendary "Pistol Pete" Maravich. In tennis, he made his mark in a white-dominated sport. By the time he was fifteen, he was already on the international stage, playing at Wimbledon.

Scholarship offers from colleges were piling up. Schools were interested in Lucas for both tennis and basketball. He chose the University of Maryland and then proceeded to do the improbable—he became an All-America in both sports.

"He would play basketball one day and start the tennis season the next,"[4] remembered Jack Zane, sports publicist for the University of Maryland.

Lucas was noticeable from the first time he walked onto a basketball court at Maryland. After *telling* everyone how great he was, he showed them. In his first game with the Terrapins, playing with such stars as Len Elmore and Tom McMillen, Lucas hit nine consecutive shots. "Luke could talk real good," Elmore said, "but he could back it up."[5]

But something was bothering Lucas.

"No matter what I achieved, I never knew when it was good enough," Lucas said. "I think I was trying to be perfect—in my daily life and on the tennis or basketball court."[6]

Teammates remember Lucas as fiercely competitive, but always ready to break up tension around the locker room with a joke or a prank. "John was effervescent, always very bubbling, a character," McMillen recalled.[7]

It was the day before a big game with North Carolina. Lucas came to practice wearing a stretch bandage on his knee. A student from the campus radio station asked Lucas if he had a problem. Feigning pain, Lucas said he wasn't sure if he could play against the Tar Heels. Excited, the student announcer rushed back with his big story. The next day, the phone was ringing non-stop in Zane's office. What was wrong with Lucas? Zane had trouble convincing everyone that Lucas was healthy and that it was just a joke.

Lucas had no fear. Lefty Driesell, the Maryland coach, was a large, intimidating presence with a booming voice. While his teammates stood by in respectful awe of their coach, the free-spirited Lucas cracked jokes. He loved to address McMillen, soon to be a Rhodes scholar, as "Senator McMillen." And years later, McMillen did become a U.S. congressman.

It seemed everything came easy to Lucas.

Six-foot-three point guards aren't usually selected as No. 1 in the NBA draft. But in 1976, Lucas was made the top pick by the Houston Rockets. Now he was a millionaire.

But something was wrong. Secretly, he wrestled with his own demons. "I kept asking what was next," Lucas said. "I'd grown up so fast in athletics that when I got to the professional ranks, I ran out of goals. Being the number one draft pick made me ask: 'Where do I go from here? There's got to be a number higher than one! The next step is death!' "[8] Lucas was about to sink into his personal, self-made hell.

When he started playing in the pros, he competed with basketball players he had idolized. By his second year, he was bored. "It stopped being a game and became a job," he said.[9]

Lucas found he had a lot of time on his hands, especially when the Rockets were on the road. He started to experiment with drugs. He had to be "the biggest and best cokehead and alcoholic in the league."[10]

If someone had "primo" cocaine, Lucas was going to get some better. If you drank two beers, he would drink three. Party to 6 A.M.? Lucas would party to 6:05. He was driven to compete, always had been, at all costs.

Lucas's wife, Debbie, first noticed his decline a few years into his NBA career. Lucas would stay out until all hours. He would say he was drinking. Debbie Lucas already knew her husband liked to drink. "I started to notice other things, like his eyes and the dryness around his mouth."[11] She had now identified signs of substance abuse.

So much of Lucas's life had been centered around winning and losing. Now he was starting to lose more than just games. He was losing his self-respect. After a while, his marriage seemed all but lost. There were times when Debbie Lucas despaired and thought about leaving her husband. But then she thought about how little John-John would crawl into bed beside his drug-saturated father. The little boy would "hold his daddy, putting his arms around him as if his daddy was the child and he was the adult."[12]

One day, Lucas's daughter Tarvia came home

from Christian school. Seeing her father in a drug- and drink-induced stupor, she blurted out: "Daddy, I am a gift from God, and you should be held liable."[13] The family was suffering, and so was Lucas's career.

The Rockets thought Lucas would be their star point guard, one of their franchise players for years to come. He could be brilliant. Once he had an astounding 14 assists in one quarter of a game. But as brilliant as Lucas could be on a basketball court, it did not overshadow the vicious cycle that had developed in his life. He checked in and out of rehabilitation centers, always with the promise that he would reform.

No such luck. He struggled to keep his job in the NBA. He drifted from team to team—at one point, he played for five teams in a five-year period. Lucas was extremely talented, but at the same time he seemed to be self-destructive.

Debbie Lucas took drastic measures: She locked her husband in the house and hid the keys.

On a night in March 1986, ten years after he had been made the No. 1 pick in the NBA draft, Lucas was about to hit the lowest point of his life. He found the keys to the house. Unlocking the door, he ran out without putting his shoes on. All he was wearing was a suit, sunglasses, and five pairs of sweat socks.

His frightened wife raced after him, afraid of what he might do.

"I drove after him with the kids, but he ran a red light," Debbie Lucas remembered. "I figured if he wanted to kill himself like that, I couldn't stop him. He was on his own."[14]

Lucas went on a drinking and drug-taking spree. He blacked out. When he awoke, he was still wearing his shades, and his elegant designer suit was soaked with his own urine. He never made practice that day. The Rockets, who had re-hired him in 1984, suspended him for the second and last time after he tested positive on a drug screening.

Until that point, Lucas had been having his best season in the NBA and the Rockets were on their way to winning their division. Lucas was devastated. He had nothing else. Competition was his way of life. He had reached bottom.

"Something happened that night that said: 'I have had enough.' "[15]

March 14, 1986, was the turning point. He checked into the Van Nuys (California) Community Hospital for rehabilitation. He was determined not to fail. "I was ready to surrender and admit that this is bigger than me," he said. "I had to accept that I have a disease."[16]

Losing all control had frightened him. When he left the hospital, he was no longer cocky. He was no longer playing basketball, so his identity was challenged. There wasn't a drug-recovery program to support him. And then there were the dreams. Recurring nightmares, where he was high on cocaine. He was more scared now than ever. His hospital support system was gone, and he realized that no professional sport had an aftercare program for alcoholics or drug abusers. One was needed, so he started knocking on doors.

But he was such a high risk that no one gave him a chance.

Then he met A. Joyce Bossett, a health-care executive at Houston International Hospital. She agreed to his recovery program, provided she supervised his aftercare. "I wanted to save my life," Lucas said, "but I also wanted to help other people. I didn't want anybody to have to go through what I did."[17] Result: the John Lucas Aftercare Treatment and Recovery Center in Houston.

It was time to restart his basketball career. He returned to the game the following year and played until 1990, completely free of drugs and alcohol. When Lucas retired after fourteen years, he had scored 9,951 points and ranked ninth on the all-time assist list. He had played for six teams, including the Houston Rockets twice.

He expanded his interests: a hospital treatment center, a fitness program, and a home for recovering addicts. Lucas inspired and became a consultant for the newly established NBA drug program.

"He would go anywhere to get someone, into crack houses and police stations,"[18] said Kevin Mackey, a basketball coach helped by Lucas's program. If someone couldn't afford the program, Lucas would dip into his own pocket to help defray the cost.

When players complained that it was difficult to make the transition back to the real world, it sparked another Lucas idea. He bought a team—the Miami Tropics of the United States Basketball League. It became the halfway house of basketball. Most coaches are concerned with winning.

Lucas was more concerned with helping the players get their lives in order. He became their coach.
Lucas wasn't in it to win a championship trophy,
but the Tropics did.

Lucas now was fast-breaking through life;
rather than slowing down after retiring from basketball, he was picking up speed. When the offer
to coach the San Antonio Spurs came in 1992,
Lucas could not resist. He felt he had been helping everybody else until now. "This is something
I did for me."[19]

Lucas's style was unorthodox. He gave his players unheard-of freedom, letting them diagram
plays during time-out huddles and allowing veterans to make personnel decisions. "I gave them
loose reins, with a lot of structure," Lucas said.
"They had to begin to believe in each other."[20] His
practices were painfully intense, yet always tem-
pered with humor.

Who would expect a coach to do a Michael
Jackson "moonwalk" during a break in practice?
The San Antonio Spurs were laughing themselves
silly one day when Lucas performed for them.
Then the Spurs performed for him. They made a
miraculous turnaround. After going 9–11 with
Tarkanian, they won 21 of their next 24. They
finished with a 39–22 record and eliminated the
Portland Trail Blazers in the first round of the
playoffs.

Even so, Lucas's unorthodox coaching came
under criticism—particularly when he gave special privileges to Dennis Rodman. Lucas allowed
the free-spirited Rodman to miss team meetings

Orchestrating from the sidelines at Philadelphia.
(Philadelphia 76ers)

and practices. Rodman thrived in the environment, but it caused morale problems. Despite a solid 94–49 record over two seasons, Lucas stepped down during a management shakeup.

He wasn't out of a job long. The Philadelphia 76ers hired Lucas in 1994. He became their coach and general manager. No one expected miracles. The 76ers had been one of the NBA's doormats for many years. As it turned out, Lucas eventually left the troubled 76ers.

No matter. Lucas had already achieved his miracle. One in a lifetime was plenty.

5

REGGIE MILLER

Reggie Miller never met a challenge he didn't like. But this time it seemed hopeless. The Indiana Pacers, down by six points, were 18.7 seconds away from losing the first game of the NBA's 1995 Eastern Conference semifinal series against the New York Knicks.

"When you're down by six with fifteen, twenty seconds left, it doesn't look good," Miller said. "But you can never give up."[1] Miller was thinking that if the Pacers could hit a quick 3-pointer, they would have a chance.

So, guess what?

Miller received the inbounds pass, turned, and fired. The ball swished through for a 3-pointer with 16.4 seconds left. The Knicks' lead was down to three.

The sellout Madison Square Garden crowd, which had been celebrating only moments earlier, was suddenly concerned.

The Knicks had the ball, but Anthony Mason was having problems getting it inbounds against the high-pressure Indiana defense. It was at that moment Miller knew he had a chance for a steal.

Pacing the Pacers. *(Indiana Pacers)*

Mason was desperately looking for an open man. He found one—Greg Anthony. Only, Anthony wasn't there after Mason fired the ball. Somehow, the Knicks' guard had fallen down on the court, and the ball ended up in Miller's hands.

After stealing the inbounds pass, Miller quickly stepped behind the 3-point line and hit another shot.

The crowd was stunned. Tie score: 105–105.

The Knicks again had the chance to put the game away. John Starks was at the foul line, but he missed both shots. Knicks center Patrick Ewing snared the rebound and missed a short jumper.

Enter Reggie Miller. The outside shooting threat was suddenly an inside man. As a guard who did most of his work shooting from the outside, the stick-thin, 6-foot-7 Miller didn't usually battle the beefy behemoths under the boards. But there he was, grabbing a rebound. And getting fouled.

Miller stepped to the line and calmly hit two shots, giving him an incredible eight points in just nine seconds. The Pacers pulled out a stunning 107–105 victory.

Everyone in the Garden was shocked, including Pacers coach Larry Brown. He was in a "state of disbelief because I never imagined that one. . . . I can't remember something like that."[2]

It wasn't anything new for Miller—he'd been supplying that kind of last-minute heroics for many years. In college, Miller was always the Last-Minute Man for UCLA. He had developed an exquisite shot in heated backyard competition with his brothers and sister, and in exhausting practice sessions where he competed with himself.

But until he became a basketball star, Miller had to learn to walk before he could run. Literally.

Reggie Miller was born with pronated hips, which forced his ankles inward. He wore braces on both legs for the first four years of his life, and then special shoes after that. For nearly a year, his mother woke him every hour during the night to change his position in bed. Doctors told Carrie Miller her son would never walk on his own. She didn't believe them.

"I didn't accept negative things," she said. "They didn't even enter my mind."[3]

But it was hard for Reggie Miller to accept his condition. Reggie had another birth defect, as well: an open chest cavity. His medicine? Liver—ugh!—twice a day. When Reggie grew up, he refused to eat liver again.

Reggie was stuck in the house with his mom and the dog. He thought of himself as a real "mama's boy." He sat at the kitchen window and watched his older brothers, Saul and Darrell, and sister, Cheryl, play basketball in the driveway. He wanted to hang out with his brothers and sister and have fun. His mother tried to cheer him up.

"She'd always say, 'You'll be out there soon, honey. You just got to get your legs stronger.' She was so optimistic. My parents never told me anything negative. They told me, 'You will walk. You will run. You will play basketball.' "[4]

Once he did start playing, Reggie had a lot of

catching up to do—and not necessarily with his brothers. "Overcoming my sister's shadow has been the biggest obstacle of my life,"[5] Reggie said. Cheryl Miller would be recognized as the greatest player in the woman's game. Reggie was known as "Cheryl's little brother."

Sports Illustrated had taunted Reggie Miller as "the first Bruin in history who couldn't beat his sister in one-on-one." Even when he became a star at UCLA and the Bruins visited other gyms, Reggie heard the taunts. As he stood at the free-throw line, they chanted, "Cher-yl, Cher-yl."

At first it bothered Reggie. Then his father taught him to use such derisive chants as motivation. Later, in the pros, he thrived on it.

When young Reggie finally got well enough to play basketball with his siblings, he worked hard. "My whole goal was to beat Cheryl."[6] If he couldn't beat her, he would join her. The two wandered around their neighborhood looking for other kids to hustle.

This was usually the scenario:

Reggie and Cheryl would look for two guys on a basketball court, already warmed up. Cheryl would hide nearby while Reggie went up to them and asked if they wanted to play two-on-two for $5 or $10.

The guys would look at Reggie's skinny body and chuckle. "Sure, who's your partner?" That was a signal for the equally frail-looking Cheryl to come dashing onto the court, pigtails flying.

The guys thought: *Easy money.* They thought differently once Cheryl and Reggie started to play. "We knew we were going for hamburgers and ice cream within the hour," Reggie remembered.[7]

The two-on-two backyard games with Cheryl and his brothers were more competitive. There, the spindly-legged Reggie and Cheryl would challenge older brothers Darrell and Saul Jr. in fierce battles. More than money was at stake here, something more important: family pride.

In these games, Reggie developed his patented jump shot from long range. He had no choice. It was the only way he could get the ball over his taller brothers, who stuffed the ball in his face every time he would try to get a shot off inside.

"Reggie always found a way to get it done," Darrell says. "He'd shoot this high, arcing jump shot. It's indicative of the way he plays now."[8]

Reggie would never miss an opportunity to practice his jump shot. Coming home from school every day, he would immediately head for the backyard basketball court that had been installed by his father, Saul.

"My father had a little area of concrete for our backyard basket," Miller recalled. "My first goal was to master every shot in that area. After I did that, I said, 'Dad, we need more concrete.' Eventually we had an area that went back maybe twenty-two feet from the basket. Any more than that was in my mother's rose garden, and I shot from there, too. I apologize, but it paid off."[9] The 3-point line in the NBA was about the same distance from the basket as the rose garden had been.

People were always telling Reggie he was too skinny and too frail to make it as a basketball player. He never argued with anyone. He just worked harder.

"People who told him he couldn't play—when they were getting out of bed in the morning, Reggie had been shooting for two or three hours," Cheryl remembered. "And when they went to bed, he was still shooting."[10]

Miller's practices paid off. He became a sensation at Riverside (California) Poly High. His first starting game as a sophomore was spectacular. He scored 39 points.

He was excited and couldn't wait to get home and tell his sister the news.

"Reggie, that's great!" Cheryl exclaimed enthusiastically.

Knowing his sister had played that night, he asked: "How did you do?"

When she answered, "I scored 105," Reggie was deflated,[11] but it provided him with the motivation to become better. He was still trying to live up to his siblings, particularly Cheryl, who had all overshadowed him as a youth.

Reggie was not one to be intimidated by physical play. High school teams would look at Reggie's 5-foot-9, thin, bony frame and believe he could be pushed around.

"I was always getting knocked down," he said, "but I would never show the other kids they hurt me. I'd get up and say, 'Is that your best shot? Come on, hit me harder!' "[12]

"He could take it," remembered Mike Bree,

coach of Riverside North, Riverside Poly's main rival. "You couldn't get too physical, because he would give it back."[13]

Miller would sometimes retaliate verbally. He began "trash-talking" as a method of self-defense. "I think trash-talking jacks me up," Miller said of the popular sports practice of verbally abusing opponents. "It gives me security."[14]

Trash-talking was the last thing you'd expect from a member of the Miller family. Reggie's father was a military man and instilled military-like discipline in the household. The Millers were religious and went to church every Sunday. Reggie knew by the tone of his voice whenever his dad was pleased.

"If he said, 'Hey, Reg,' I'd say, 'Yeah, Dad,' and if he said, 'Reginald,' it was always, 'Yes, sir.' I was so scared of my parents that if I did anything wrong, my conscience would kill me."[15]

Cheryl was already a big star at Southern Cal when Reggie decided to go to UCLA. As if there weren't enough of a rivalry within the family, brother and sister were now playing at two schools that were among the fiercest rivals in sports. However, Reggie was beginning to make his own mark.

Walt Hazzard, the new coach at UCLA, was excited. He had spent hours and hours looking at videotapes of the team from the previous season. "One of the things that jumped out was Reggie Miller: his competitiveness, his quickness. He had a style and a spirit I thought was incredible. On top of everything, he had a shot and a range with that shot that I had never seen before."[16]

Hazzard summoned Miller into his office for a private meeting. "You know, you are going to be a very rich man," he said to his startled sophomore.

"What do you mean?" Reggie asked.

"You are going to make millions and millions of dollars playing this game. You are going to be a superstar."

"Me?"

"Yeah," Hazzard said. "Here are the rules: I want you to understand that you have the greenest light I have ever given to a basketball player. I don't care where you shoot the ball from. I only tell you, when you miss, don't look at me. Just prepare yourself to shoot the next shot."[17]

Miller was like a kid with a new toy, beside himself with joy. No coach had ever given him that kind of green light. Why, just the year before as a little-used freshman, hadn't he been criticized for taking "bad" shots from too far out? As far as Hazzard was concerned, Miller couldn't take enough. It took a while before Miller got accustomed to this newfound freedom in games—then it was bombs away.

"The most important thing was that he had developed the self-assuredness and confidence that was unmatched," Hazzard said.[18]

No player was more beloved at UCLA, or more hated by the Bruins' opponents. Along with his shooting, Miller brought the trash-talking part of his game to a new level—lower, rather than higher, some said. He was highly vocal and demonstrative on the court, never shy about showing up an opponent or an official. When he fouled out of one game against Arizona, Miller rubbed his fingers together in a sign indicating "payola"—a suggestion that the official was being paid off to make sure that UCLA lost. Another favorite Reggie sign: clutching his throat with both hands, as if to indicate that the opponents, or officials, were "choking"—losing their composure in a critical situation.

"I'll admit that sometimes I get carried away," Miller said. "Sometimes you wish you could turn back the hands of the clock and have a chance to do something differently. That's usually stuff that has to do with the officials."[19]

Even though Reggie was on his way to becoming the second-leading scorer in UCLA history, he was still having a hard time keeping up with his sister. Her accomplishments included two national championships at USC and a gold medal in the Olympics. Reggie was motivated by an article in *Sports Illustrated* that said he couldn't compete with his sister.

"That's when I started to kick it into overdrive," Reggie said. "We started winning games."[20] With the red-hot Miller shooting nearly 60 percent, UCLA won the National Invitational Tournament and he was named Most Outstanding Player. It was the first of many great performances for him at Madison Square Garden in New York. The following season, Miller became a bona fide All-America candidate and challenged his sister for space on the sports pages.

The Pacers made Miller their No. 1 choice in the 1987 NBA draft. He became a popular figure in Indiana and a compelling figure around the league as he enhanced the art of jump shooting.

"The common denominator among shooters is that we all worked hard to develop our shot," Miller says. "I don't think kids do that today. These days, you don't go to the playground to shoot your J. You go to try to dunk on someone's head. I did that, too, but I always brought my jump shot with me."[21]

Even before Miller burned them in the 1995 play-offs, the New York Knicks were well aware of Miller's explosiveness. In a playoff game the year before, he had scored a remarkable 25 points in the last quarter to help the Pacers pull out a 93–86 victory. He made five 3-point baskets in that dazzling finish, including one shot from twenty-seven feet that swished through without touching the rim. It was like "somebody drops the ball straight down from the center of the arena,"[22] said Pacers president Donnie Walsh, who as a scout originally recommended Miller for the team.

Miller gives his opponents problems in other ways. As former Knick Derek Harper has observed, "When it comes to getting under people's skin, nobody can touch him."[23]

Sometimes, Reggie doesn't have to say a word to infuriate his opponents. After releasing a shot,

Reggie got the green light at UCLA. *(UCLA)*

he has a habit of keeping his right arm extended in the air for a few seconds. Opponents regard this as showboating. Miller does not.

"I don't do that to taunt anyone," he says. "I do it because when my father taught me to shoot, he taught me to extend that arm and keep it up there real high. That's how you assure yourself that you're following through."[24]

Miller also keeps his eyes on the ball, rather than the basket.

"I can see the rotation, the way it looks in the air, and maybe learn something for the next shot."[25]

He doesn't mind that he is perhaps the most hated player in arenas around the NBA. Except, of course, in Indianapolis. He has a strong fan base not only at Market Square Arena but also in children's hospitals, where he is a frequent visitor. "I understand what it's like for a kid to be trapped inside behind four walls," he said.[26]

He thrives in confrontational circumstances with opposing fans.

"That's the best, when they bring [insulting] signs and cards," Miller said. "That means all day they were thinking, *What am I going to do to harass Reggie Miller?* I don't resent being booed or when they yell, 'Cheryl, Cheryl.' It motivates me when they yell at me. I love playing on the road. It's where I live."[27]

In the summer of 1995, Miller was picked for "Dream Team III," which would represent the United States in the 1996 Olympics. Miller fans figured he was due for recognition: He had averaged 19.3 points a game in eight years in the NBA.

But the ultimate recognition as far as Miller was concerned could have come during an incident at a Los Angeles nightclub. Sister Cheryl was trying to get into the club, which was packed beyond packed. Everyone in L.A., it seemed, had been trying to get in, but to no avail.

Cheryl told the bouncer who she was: You know, Cheryl Miller of All-America and Olympic gold medal fame? The bouncer just shrugged.

"You'll have to stand in line with everyone else," he told the chagrined Cheryl.

Finally, someone in line piped up: "That's Reggie Miller's sister."[28]

Those were the magic words. She was ushered in immediately.

6

HAKEEM OLAJUWON

Hakeem Olajuwon was shivering. Dressed in his traditional lightweight clothing, the 6-foot-11 Nigerian teenager had just arrived at John F. Kennedy Airport in New York. It was only October, but unseasonably cold winds were howling outside. Dare he venture out? He stared down at his list. St. John's University was to be his first stop. Too cold. He took the next plane. Destination: Houston.

The phone rang on Guy Lewis's desk at the University of Houston's basketball office.

"Hello, Coach, this is Hakeem!"

"Hakeem who?" asked the Cougars basketball coach.

"Hakeem . . . Hakeem Olajuwon. I'm from Africa. You've heard about me?"

Lewis had heard about Olajuwon. One of his assistants mirrored Lewis's thoughts when he blurted: "Oh, Coach, not another foreign player that can't play!"[1]

No one was excited. No one even wanted to go to the Houston airport to pick him up. Lewis had

---

Hakeem Olajuwon reached for greatness at the University of Houston. *(University of Houston)*

been skeptical when a scout told him about this "young giant" in Africa.

"He told me he was six foot seven, and I figured that would be six-three. That's just the way it usually goes. So I was expecting a six-three guy from Africa. I wasn't expecting much."[2]

Much later, as one of the assistants glanced out the window, a cab pulled up. Olajuwon started to get out. Excited at what he was seeing, the assistant called to the others. They came running to see the new recruit. It seemed as if Hakeem just kept coming out of the cab. "Instead of being six-three—or even six-seven—he was six-eleven," Lewis said.[3] They all looked at each other in disbelief and then rushed out to greet him.

Hakeem looked like a basketball player. There was only one problem—he couldn't play basketball. To call him raw would be putting it mildly.

When he first saw the eighteen-year-old Olajuwon, "he had played a total of three months of basketball in his life," remembered Lewis. "Any junior high school player in America has more experience than that."[4]

Fast-forward to the 1994 NBA finals, where Olajuwon was about to face the biggest challenge of his career: Hakeem vs. Patrick Ewing in the Battle of the Superstar Centers. It was hard to believe he was the same raw player who had arrived on the campus of the University of Houston in 1981 with stars in his eyes and a dream. The only things he had going for him then were his height and his heart.

"The Project," as Olajuwon was called at the University of Houston, was about to begin. . . .

In Africa, basketball was not a primary sport. Soccer was.

"They don't show you basketball on [Nigerian] TV," Olajuwon said.[5]

Since he was a little boy he had played goaltender on soccer teams, because nobody ever wanted the position. In his own words, he was a "real good goalie." He loved the excitement of it, loved being in the middle of the action and blocking those zipping, bulletlike shots. He also participated in team handball, which was played by passing a ball up and down a field and trying to score by throwing the ball into an undersized soccer net.

Starring on the high school soccer team, Olajuwon literally stood head and shoulders above everyone else. Cat-quick and agile, his long, angular frame filled the net and intimidated opponents. "They would go away scared," Olajuwon remembers with vivid amusement.[6]

Olajuwon was several inches taller than most youngsters his age, in some ways a freak among his people. His unusual height made him an easy target. Schoolmates and neighborhood boys constantly taunted him. Olajuwon wound up getting into many fights.

He felt ashamed to be different. Why did he have to be so tall? He wished he were a normal height. Then he could be "friendly just like everybody else,"[7] and not constantly defending himself. But Olajuwon didn't feel different on an athletic field, although his parents thought sports were a waste of time. Olajuwon would have to sneak out of the house to play his games.

At least it kept him off the streets in Lagos, a crowded, thriving city on the west coast of Africa, not unlike New York. Lagos was frightening in some ways when Olajuwon was growing up in the 1970s. When he was a teenager, two military coups rocked the country. Many lives were lost.

"They were killing people at the top of the government on their way to work," Olajuwon remembers. "If you were going to work, you might mistakenly get hurt. So everybody went back home."[8]

In this ominous climate, sports was a way of focusing on positive things. Olajuwon was seventeen years old when a schoolmate introduced him to basketball, a relatively new game in Africa. Until then, Olajuwon had thought basketball was like "netball," a game played by African girls with a net but no backboard. Olajuwon stood at the foul line to see if he could shoot free throws. After several misses, Olajuwon finally hit one. He was hooked.

"Once I started playing basketball, I didn't play those other sports again," Olajuwon says.[9]

If Olajuwon needed any further convincing, he got it from Richard Mills, a San Diego man who was coach of the Nigerian national basketball team. Mills enlisted Hakeem for his squad.

Even though he had to learn the rules of this new game, Olajuwon had been prepared well by other sports. Soccer had made his legs strong, handball had given him coordination, and track and field had given him stamina. But none of the sports taught him how to dunk a basketball.

In his first important game for the Nigerian national team, Olajuwon found out how frustrating basketball could be. In the closing seconds, he was under the basket as he caught a pass from a teammate. He leaped into the air and tried to push the ball into the basket. To his embarrassment, he missed.

"I didn't know how to dunk," he says. "And I couldn't lay it up, either. I didn't know how to use the glass. I was so mad . . . we lost the game. I thought at the time, *I give up, I don't want to play this game anymore.*"[10]

But he didn't give up.

Christopher Pond, a U.S. state department worker coaching in Africa, convinced Olajuwon that he had a future as a basketball player in America. He arranged for Olajuwon to visit several colleges in the United States, including the University of Houston.

Olajuwon wanted to go to America, and this was one way to do it—a basketball scholarship. He had been thinking about going abroad since he was a young boy. It was a status symbol in his country.

In the 1950s, an oil boom transformed Nigeria from a third-world country into one with a world-

class economy. Many of the citizens, now afflu-
ent, sent their children abroad for an education.
The United States was considered trendy.

"The first time I ever thought about it, I was
eight or nine years old," Olajuwon said. "At that
time, I didn't understand the significance of
going to school overseas or what it meant to come
to America."[11]

His mother, who ran a cement business in
Lagos, had hoped her son would study abroad
and return home to find a job—much like his
older brother, Kaka, who was educated in London
and became a government surveyor in Lagos.

That was the practical view. Hakeem, however,
had a vision of his own.

"In Nigeria, I had a special feeling inside of
me," he said. "Something was going to happen."
Olajuwon felt he had something that no one else
had, and when it was time, "I knew my road was
going to be in sports."[12]

So Olajuwon arrived in America.

"The day I arrived in New York, it was cold,"
Olajuwon remembered, "so I went on to Houston,
where, I was told, it was warm."[13]

At first, Olajuwon was a curiosity at the University of Houston. A graceful and elegant giant, he
walked across campus dressed in his vivid, flow-
ing native garb. He was hard to miss. A coaching assistant brought him over to meet the
basketball team. Teammate David Rose would
never forget the scene.

"He was dressed in this embroidered white suit
from top to bottom, a long dress with pants, and

a bright, white cap with the same embroidery, and he was wearing sandals. I went to shake his hand, to introduce myself. He bowed and said he was glad to meet me. He was bowing to all of his teammates."[14]

It was a mark of respect in Olajuwon's homeland.

"I was brought up to honor older people," Olajuwon said. "Okay, they laughed at me—so I stopped."[15]

On campus, Olajuwon felt out of place in other ways. There was still some ignorance in Houston about Africans, and Olajuwon encountered thoughtless prejudice. When he first came to Houston, he was an outsider—taunted by some because he was African. He spoke with a thick English accent that sometimes made it difficult to communicate.

"I know some people still think I was living in Nigeria, naked in the jungle and swinging through the trees," Olajuwon said. "I know what they think about Africa. I do not like it. Lagos is a big, vibrant city."[16]

Many of the students at the University of Houston would perhaps have been surprised to learn just how sophisticated Olajuwon was. He could speak English and French and four Nigerian dialects, and he had traveled extensively. None of this was immediately evident to his classmates, however. During his first year at Houston, he was quiet and his most used expression was "I don't understand."[17] And he missed African food. He was hungry, always hungry. At 190 pounds, he was told to fill out, but there was nothing to eat—at first.

Soon he discovered hamburgers and ice cream.

"We had a McDonald's across the street from the gym," Rose recalled, "and when Olajuwon first got to Houston, he'd be up there in the stands watching practice and he'd have a grocery sack. I didn't know McDonald's made bags that big. It was just stuffed with food."[18]

Soon Olajuwon was eating T-bone steaks and ice cream. Walking around campus, he carried his own cooler filled with ice cream. The new diet, combined with strenuous workouts in the gym, eventually enabled him to build his body into a more athletic 250 pounds.

"Nobody really thought he was going to be much of an impact player, because he was very thin," Rose recalled. "Then he started to gain weight. That was one of the things that was really amazing, how strong physically he became so quickly. He was on that Big Mac diet."[19]

Although Olajuwon became Americanized rather quickly, it took him longer to shape up as a basketball player.

"The first time I saw him play was in an old gym, the physical education building," Rose remembered. "He was in a noontime league with a bunch of college professors. You could tell he had a lot of athletic ability, but some of those college professors were actually getting more done than he was."[20]

Because of his limited knowledge of basketball,

Olajuwon was not easy to teach. But Coach Guy Lewis loved his dedication. "If a player didn't care, you might lose interest. But in his case, he was right there wanting to know more. How? Why? He'd ask questions."[21]

There was no rush to find a place for him in the Houston Cougars lineup. Olajuwon was "redshirted"—kept off the roster for his first year—so that he could learn the fundamentals of the game.

Redshirted! Olajuwon burst into tears. He thought he wouldn't be allowed to play basketball. His coach explained that the "redshirt" designation allows an athlete to compete for four years after sitting out his first year.

Olajuwon was molded in the fiery cauldron of Cougar practices: "red" team vs. "white" team. Three hours a day. Twenty-minute games at a time. Winner takes a rest. Loser takes laps. Olajuwon was such a newcomer to basketball, he would constantly take a ferocious beating in practices from the Cougars' big men. He was already in pain, suffering from back spasms. It seemed Olajuwon spent nearly as much time at team practices hanging upside down in a gravity machine as shooting basketballs.

As a freshman, Olajuwon had other problems: He was fouling out of games too quickly. He was miserable. He started thinking he couldn't play the game. Coach Lewis made life more miserable for him by talking about all his faults with reporters. Naturally, this made headlines and made

Olajuwon very unhappy. One day a tearful Olajuwon showed up on Lewis's doorstep. He was hurt by Lewis's comments to the press.

But not hurt enough to discourage him from improving himself. He found refuge during the summer. His basketball education accelerated when he played at the Fonde Recreation Center in Houston against NBA all-star Moses Malone and other top players. Olajuwon found an oasis at the recreation center. There, he could be himself. And he found a friend in Malone.

"It was the best thing he could have done, playing with Moses all summer," said Robert Reid, another NBA player who competed with Olajuwon during those no-holds-barred summer games at Fonde. "You could tell the difference in Hakeem every week. He really didn't know his own strength when he first started playing with us."[22]

By the end of the summer of 1982, Olajuwon was a "power" player. Instead of being awed by Malone, one of the NBA's greatest players, he was challenging him, trying to block shots and going right at him on offense.

One day at a Cougars practice during the 1982–83 season, Lewis was startled. He turned to his assistants.

"Do you see what I'm seeing?"[23]

Olajuwon had suddenly emerged into an all-around force, and it seemed as if it had happened overnight.

"All of a sudden, he started dominating," Lewis

remembered. "I'm talking about offense. He had been helping defense, blocking shots and that kind of thing."[24]

"Phi Slama Jama" was born. It was a nickname given to the fast-breaking, slam-dunk-crazy Cougars. Olajuwon gave their backboard-rattling shots a huge exclamation point and earned his own nickname: "Hakeem the Dream."

For opponents, he was a nightmare. Olajuwon led the nation in blocked shots and averaged more than 13 points and 11 rebounds a game as the Cougars reeled off 25 straight victories on their way to the NCAA finals.

His team was favored to win by a large margin over North Carolina State. The Cougars led by six points with three minutes to go. North Carolina State came back to win on a last-second shot.

Olajuwon couldn't believe it. Tears streamed down his face at courtside.

"During my freshman year we lost four in a row," Olajuwon said later. "I can accept that. But we were playing a weaker team, and they beat us; then it really hurts."[25]

Olajuwon was named the tournament's Most Valuable Player, an honor that usually goes to someone from the winning team.

In the 1983–84 season, Clyde Drexler and Larry Micheaux had graduated, leaving the Phi Slama Jama fraternity without two key members. But it had the big gun, Olajuwon. He led another charge to the NCAA finals.

The championship game matched the country's two premier big men: Olajuwon vs. Patrick Ewing of Georgetown. Ewing won this battle, sending the Cougars home without the title for the second straight year. Lewis said, "Hakeem doesn't understand the game yet."[26]

Olajuwon thought long and hard about staying in school to complete his degree. His parents didn't understand basketball. No one in his family had ever seen a basketball game. They were waiting for him to finish his education and come back to Africa to work in the cement business.

Olajuwon made his decision. Forgoing his senior year at Houston, he joined a pool of rich collegiate talent in the 1984 NBA draft. Olajuwon was the No. 1 pick by the Houston Rockets. He was selected over a field that included Michael Jordan, Charles Barkley, and John Stockton, all of whom would eventually play on the first U.S. "Dream Team" in the Olympics.

The Rockets had been one of the NBA's worst teams the year before, winning only 29 of 82 games. Things were about to change. Olajuwon, now 7 feet, 255 pounds, teamed with seven-footer Ralph Sampson in the vaunted "Twin Towers" offense. Suddenly, the Rockets were in the playoffs. By Olajuwon's second season, they were in the NBA finals. They became a perennial playoff team—long after Sampson had left—except for the 1991–1992 season.

But a championship continued to elude Olajuwon. He had missed the NCAA title in college. As

With Olajuwon, the Houston Rockets took off. *(AP Wide World)*

he approached his tenth year in the NBA, he was still looking for his first NBA title.

"I've been close so many times," Olajuwon said. "You are judged by winning. To win a championship, that really is the only dream that matters."[27]

So much had happened to Olajuwon in that time: Contract battles with management. Battles with teammates. A serious eye injury.

He was still determined to prove his worth, and came back to win the Most Valuable Player Award in the 1993–94 season. Playing the most complete basketball of his career, he led the Rockets into the NBA finals against the New York Knicks, painted as the villains in this production. The Knicks played physical basketball—some thought a little too physical. Their hard-hitting style intimidated a lot of teams.

Olajuwon was about to face an old enemy, Knicks center Patrick Ewing. When the two had met in another championship setting, in college, Ewing had been victorious.

The Battle of the Giants was about to begin.

Olajuwon outscored and outplayed Ewing in every game. He was the high scorer in six games and tied for the honor in the seventh as he emerged with the playoff MVP Award. More important, the Rockets won their first world championship.

A repeat in 1995 would show that their title wasn't an accident. Could they do it? Sportswriters had made San Antonio center David Robinson the league MVP in 1994–95. Olajuwon finished fifth in the voting. What did Olajuwon have to do to prove he was the best center in the league? Outplay Robinson? He did exactly that. Outplay Orlando's Shaquille O'Neal? Again, no sweat.

In 1995, the Rockets won their second straight championship.

After a long and torturous journey, Hakeem had finally arrived.

7

JOHN STARKS

The supermarket was deserted. John Starks dashed down the aisle, gripping a can of pork and beans. He stopped short and leaped as high as he could. With a loud thump, he deposited the can on the tallest shelf.

Dunk shot. Two points.

As Starks headed for the back of the store, he made a standing jump. Up he went, his fingers stretched out, and scraped the ceiling light fixtures. *Thwack!* His heavy construction boots landed on the slick linoleum floor, echoing throughout the supermarket.

Starks was playing games to relieve the drudgery of the "graveyard" shift at the Safeway in Tulsa, Oklahoma. It was called a graveyard shift because you worked overnight while everyone else was sleeping.

Starks knew he had the talent to be a great basketball player. He told his coworkers he was a "natural" with a great jump shot. They laughed. What was he doing working these strange hours

Nothing could stop John Starks from taking off in the NBA. *(AP Wide World)*

in a dead-end job? Paying the bills, for one thing. But how far could you go on $3.35 an hour?

Starks was a basketball talent waiting to be discovered. The only thing was, he never stayed in one place long enough for anyone to find him. Four years, four different colleges in Oklahoma. A wife and eventually a child to support. In between college and basketball, Starks worked at odd jobs to keep food on the table.

That was before the twisty road map of this determined basketball vagabond took him through two minor professional leagues and two NBA teams. Before he became an all-star guard with the New York Knicks.

"I refused to quit," Starks said. "I knew I had enough talent to play in the NBA."[1]

There was nothing to mark John Starks as an NBA prospect when he was growing up in Tulsa. His participation in organized basketball was so minimal, it was difficult to assess his talent.

John was about seven years old when he discovered basketball. He played on his neighbors' dirt court where a slab of wood served as a backboard, with a hubcap rim as a hoop. John and his friends would jump off the trash cans and slam-dunk the basketball. He loved it from his first shot.

As John got older and everyone else was going to parties, he would be at the park, playing ball with a friend. "We'd play one-on-one from as soon as we got out of school till midnight, and if he wasn't available, I'd just go out there and shoot. I had my share of dates, but my love was basketball."[2]

Playing in the park was fun, but it didn't prepare him for organized sports. It wasn't until his junior year in high school that he finally got to play basketball on an organized level. And then it was only on the junior varsity team.

"He'd get into games and be all alone and dribble the ball off his foot," his brother Tony recalled.[3]

Then, on the high school team, he put his foot in his mouth.

Starks was playing point guard in a game for Tulsa Central and refused to take a shot as his team went down to a two-point defeat.

His coach was furious. He wanted to know why Starks hadn't taken any shots.

Starks didn't think a point guard should take shots. That's when the coach told him to take a seat on the bench for two games. The quick-tempered Starks quit, ending his organized-basketball experience in high school. Controlling his emotions was going to be a lifelong problem for Starks. He went back to the playground.

"I'd go to parks and find the high school guys who were going to be Division One college players," Starks said. "I'd play against them and dog 'em out. I got it in my mind that I could play at that level."[4] Starks did have talent. He just needed practice and more playing time. But he didn't have time for either as a senior in high school. There were more pressing needs.

One of seven children, Starks lived in poverty. His father left the family when John was three years old. Starks's mother, Irene, a nurse, and grandmother, Callie, raised the family. "They taught me valuable lessons: about life, about getting along with people, about how to survive," Starks said.[5]

Starks's growing-up years were an indication of things to come. Then, as in later years, he was always on the move. "Sometimes the rent money just wasn't there, and we had to pack up and move," said Starks, who remembered that his family changed addresses seven or eight times in Tulsa. "It was a survival test. Sometimes we'd go with one meal. We didn't have nice clothes."[6]

One of Starks's homes was typical. Two families lived in one three-bedroom house, sixteen people in all. "We used to have bunk beds stacked on top of each other, all the way up to the ceiling, so you had to slide into bed like sardines."[7]

Perhaps that explains how Starks learned to fight for space on a court and become the firecracker personality so well known to NBA fans. His brothers Vincent and Tony further toughened him up in family football games. Vincent Starks advised his younger brother: "If you want to be the best, you've got to get tough."[8]

Starks was afraid of being called a "sissy" and a "wimp" by his brothers. He took ferocious poundings in the football games—and came back for more. His mom remembered a "laid-back" John who was never the same after playing those ferocious football games with his brothers.

Life wasn't all fun and games for Starks. In his senior year in high school, instead of lifting a basketball toward the hoop, he was lifting bales of paper for $100 a week so his family could eat.

Whenever he could, he played basketball at the local recreation center or in street games.

Following high school, Starks attended local colleges. Rogers State was the first. The coach there felt Starks had "too much street ball" in his game. "They wanted to redshirt me, and I thought I was good enough to be playing. The coach didn't think so. I decided to change schools."[9]

Rather than sit out a year as a redshirt, he enrolled at Northern Oklahoma. But not for long. He played only the fall semester. Starks was hoping for a scholarship that never came. "They weren't too enthused about athletics down there," he said.[10] The final straw was a dorm discipline problem. Starks bagged school and went to Safeway to bag groceries.

He began feeling low and downhearted. Frustrated at every turn, he was discouraged. The tough day-to-day existence started to crowd out his dreams. "Instead of seeing myself in the NBA, I was wondering, 'Will I ever stop struggling?' When you're in hard, mean times, you can't think about tomorrow."[11]

"Tomorrow" turned out to be about a year and a half later, after he had worked his share of graveyard shifts. While stocking shelves, he took stock of his life. "I sat out a year because I was bored in school," Starks said, "but working at Safeway made me realize I needed to go back."[12]

Next stop: Oklahoma Junior College. Starks found an ally in Ken Trickey, one of the first basketball coaches to truly believe in his talent.

Trickey accepted the talent along with Starks's eccentric behavior.

The team bus sat idling in the parking lot, ready to take off for a rescheduled game in Independence, Kansas—a trip of about two and a half hours. Starks was missing. The engine was getting warmer and Trickey was getting hotter by the minute. Trickey's patience was wearing thin. Finally, he told the driver to go. He couldn't wait any longer.

The bus pulled out. The Oklahoma JC team would have to play this game without its AWOL star player.

The players looked lethargic after the long ride. They looked worse on the court. They couldn't have been more surprised when Starks showed up at halftime, dashing into the locker room with his bag and shoes and wearing an embarrassed grin on his face. His excuse? He had just gotten married that day. Knowing the guys were depending on him, he cut his wedding reception short to make the game.

The newlyweds made the hundred-mile trip from Tulsa in an hour and forty-five minutes, despite being stopped for a speeding ticket. What did Starks do once he got to Independence? He turned up the speed on the court, tossing in 30 points in a blazing second-half finish.

The season was a first for Starks—he actually finished the school year. And he was about to be discovered by a major university.

Leonard Hamilton was trying to rebuild the basketball program at Oklahoma State. "We kept

Starks had reason to smile at Oklahoma State. *(Oklahoma State)*

hearing about this young man who hadn't played a whole lot of ball but had a lot of athletic ability," Hamilton remembered of Starks. "So we investigated and found out that everything we'd heard about him was true."[13]

Walk into the OSU gym and there was a lone figure shooting by himself. Want to play one-on-one? Starks was always ready. Starks was an addicted basketball player, a "gym rat" who loved to practice, loved the smooth feel of the round orange ball in his hands. He seemed to be trying to make up for lost time.

Starks was an overnight sensation. He had walked into a Division I program, the highest level of college basketball, with limited experience. Yet he immediately won a position as a starting guard and had an impressive year. He led Oklahoma State in assists and steals and finished among the leaders in scoring and rebounding. His crowd-pleasing specialty was the transition game: Steal the ball and start his team on a fast break, maybe finish off the break with a slam dunk. "I remember people saying they loved to come to games just so they could see John dunk," said Bill Self, an assistant coach at Oklahoma State.[14]

Starks was expressive in other ways. He loved playing music in the locker room because it helped him prepare for games, and he was never shy about offering his opinions on coaching strategy.

The year after Starks graduated, he made a return visit during Oklahoma State's game with archrival Oklahoma. Things weren't going so well for Oklahoma State. At the half, Hamilton and his staff walked into the locker room to get the surprise of their lives. Starks was standing in front of the team, giving a pep talk.

"Uninvited, John's at the chalkboard with the marker in his hands, telling the team what we needed to do in order to win the game," Self remembered. "It was a tense moment, but I just burst out laughing. It was the funniest thing I had ever seen."[15]

During his senior year, Starks would talk to his coaches about his dreams. He dreamed of playing for Pat Riley. Pat would let him run.

Starks always felt he could play in the NBA.

Now, following his great season at Oklahoma State, he was convinced. But no NBA team drafted Starks. Each year, the NBA holds a draft to select the top players from the college ranks. The league gets a large majority of its players this way. Even if you're drafted, there's no guarantee you will make a team. But Starks was in the unenviable position of trying to make an NBA team without ever having been drafted.

He started knocking on doors. He tried out for the San Antonio Spurs. Their coach, Larry Brown, knew Starks from college. No luck.

Next stop: Golden State Warriors. Better luck there, but then disappointment. The Warriors signed him as a backup guard, but let him go after 36 games of part-time play.

"I loved him to death and still do," said Don Nelson, then the Warriors' coach. "His shot selection wasn't good and he wasn't polished, but he worked so damn hard."[16]

Starks was admittedly down, but he refused to give up. The Continental Basketball Association is a league of hopefuls and has-beens. Players are either winding up their careers there, or using it as a stepping-stone for the NBA. Starks looked upon it as an education when he joined the Cedar Rapids (Iowa) Silver Bullets.

Starks was a student of basketball, spending hours the morning after games watching films of his performance to see where he could make improvements. "The thing was not to get frustrated, know your weaknesses, and try to improve," Starks remembered of his days in the CBA.[17]

Starks was making only $550 a week, and

counting his pennies. Recalled Cedar Rapids coach George Whittaker: "He was always saying, 'Coach, you going to take care of me for lunch?' I said, 'Man, I got the same per diem you got.' I was kidding him that he might break down and buy himself a pair of shoes one day."[18]

Starks did manage to buy himself some suits to wear on road trips. He was one of the few players in the CBA to do so. He tried to present a good, clean image. It wasn't apparent on the basketball court. In a game against the Quad City Thunder, Starks displayed his formidable temper when he was called for a technical foul. Upset, he bumped the official with his chest and was fined and suspended for the remainder of the season. It scared away the Detroit Pistons, who were going to give him a tryout. A player who was such a straight shooter, Starks had shot himself in the foot.

"This was just a little setback," Starks later recalled of the incident. "I had no doubt I'd make it someday."[19]

Despite Starks's elite status as a CBA all-star, the NBA was still out of reach. But it was not out of Starks's dreams. He turned down a lucrative offer to play in Europe. His inner voice was saying: *If I go to Europe, people will forget me here.*

After playing in the low-profile World Basketball League and in a summer league in Los Angeles, Starks found himself back in the NBA. But it wasn't expected to be a long stay. The New York Knicks needed a practice player in training camp, and Starks was the man. "He wasn't afraid to stick his nose in there and fight if he had to," remembered Al Bianchi, at that time general manager of the Knicks. "I rolled the dice with the bonus money [$25,000], but I knew he was one tough scrapper."[20]

As much as Bianchi loved Starks's energetic play, the Knicks were overloaded with guards. Starks was due to be cut.

"With nothing to lose"[21] at the end of training camp, Starks drove the lane with his accustomed abandon, heading straight at Patrick Ewing. Starks, a full half-foot shorter than the Knicks' 7-foot, all-star center, tried to launch himself over Ewing for a dunk shot. But Ewing hammered Starks to the floor, causing the young hopeful to suffer a severely strained knee.

What seemed like a bad break turned into good luck for Starks. He was placed on the injured list and the Knicks could not release him. During the season, guard Trent Tucker went down, and guess who replaced him on the roster? Starks.

Several years later, after Starks had established himself as a clutch performer in the NBA, the "tough scrapper" description by Bianchi was never more appropriate. Starks played with broken noses. He came back from knee surgery to star in the playoffs. A combative player, he symbolized the "new" New York Knicks under Pat Riley, his "dream coach."

Starks, only the third CBA player to participate in the NBA All-Star Game, continues to play with desperation. He appreciates how hard it is to get to the NBA.

8

ISIAH THOMAS

Isiah Thomas was shaking.

Twenty-five members of the Vice Lords stood on his front porch. They were there to recruit the Thomas boys for their gang. When they decided you were in, you were in. No one said no to the Vice Lords. They terrorized K-Town, a west side Chicago neighborhood.

Mary Thomas answered the door.

"We want your boys," demanded the leader of the gang, a pistol bulging out of his waistband. "They're old enough to join us."[1]

The feisty little woman stared back. "There's only one gang around here," she snapped. "That's the Thomas gang, and I lead that." The gang leader held his ground.

Angrily, Mary Thomas walked back to her bedroom, returning with a shotgun.

"Get off my porch, or I'll blow you 'cross the expressway."

The Vice Lords never returned to menace the Thomas family. The image of that scene returned vividly to Isiah Thomas time and again as he rose to basketball prominence, first as a player and

Isiah puts it into high gear for the Pistons. *(AP Wide World)*

then in management in the National Basketball Association.

"If my mother hadn't been so tough, she wouldn't have made it," said Thomas, now vice president and general manager of the expansion team Toronto Raptors. "Our family would not have made it. I would not have made it."[2]

Tough, with a heart—that's what they said about Mary Thomas. Isiah was like his mom as he struggled up from Chicago's mean streets to the high roads of basketball. Few would have given Isiah Thomas, the youngest of nine children, much of a chance to survive his ghetto setting. This harsh life was a factor that led his father to leave the family when Isiah was only three. Before he left, he encouraged the children in their studies and emphasized the need for them to stick together for survival.

"He would gather seven sticks and put them in a bunch and tell us, 'It's a lot harder to break seven sticks together than one at a time,' " recalled Preston Thomas, one of the seven Thomas brothers.[3]

As the only parent, Mary Thomas did all she could to keep the family together and keep her children in line. She was a small woman with a heart condition, but she was the toughest one in the family.

"She used to whup us with the ironing cord" if anyone needed discipline, Preston Thomas remembered. Once when Isiah was caught stealing fruit from a neighborhood supermarket, he pleaded, "Call the police, but PLEASE don't call my mother!"[4]

Perhaps Isiah could be excused for stealing fruit. Many times, he felt hunger pangs in his stomach because he did not have enough to eat.

"Food was rarely in our house. We got food from the church, and one time that was all Hamburger Helper. Boxes and boxes of Hamburger Helper. No hamburger, just the helper. We ate that, like, forever. When Quaker Oats came out with their granola, they gave a lot of it away. My mother used to get all that granola and bring it home. We never had milk or anything. We'd just eat granola until we got full."[5]

Mary Thomas was giving away what little she had. Anyone in need could expect a handout from this big-hearted lady who regarded her entire neighborhood as "family" and her neighbors as "sons and daughters."

Her generosity extended to friends and foes alike. Once when Willie Lord, leader of the dreaded Vice Lords, was thrown in jail, Mary Thomas scraped together all her savings to post bail for him. Unfortunately, it came on the first of the month—rent payment day. There was no money left for the rent. Isiah and his family were forced to leave their home and live with relatives.

Isiah wasn't always assured of a place to sleep in his own home. "If I didn't sleep with my mother, I'd sleep on the floor in the closet between my brothers' and sisters' bedrooms. And we had a lot of strays coming through our house. It was like my mother was running a halfway house, so anybody could stay, and my spaces would be taken. A lot of times I slept on the ironing board in the hall."[6]

Isiah's determination and brashness as a basketball player could be traced to his mother. One day an infuriated Mary Thomas marched into the office of Chicago mayor Richard Daley, unannounced, to complain about her housing situation. A social worker threatened to withhold her welfare check if she did not move her family into the projects, a lower-income housing development where crime was rampant.

The mayor listened to Mary Thomas and told her, "Now, go on back home." He didn't make any promises. About two hours later, she received her welfare check.[7]

Mary Thomas's stand on principles was impressive. After all, a welfare check was her major means of support. She also worked in the cafeteria of Our Lady of Sorrows grade school and ran its youth program. Isiah drew attention for his basketball antics at Our Lady of Sorrows. Isiah had been the fans' favorite for many years. As a three-year-old, he would provide halftime entertainment at basketball games.

"We gave Isiah an old jersey that fell like a dress on him, and he wore black oxfords and tossed up shots with a high arc," remembered his brother Alexis, who coached the Our Lady of Sorrows team. "At three, he could shoot the eyes out of the basket."[8]

One of Isiah's favorite haunts was Gladys Park,

two blocks from his home on Congress Street. It had a small, pockmarked basketball court and a sandbox. Isiah was starting to learn the sport.

"You could always get a game there," he remembered, "any time of day, any time of night. Me and my brothers used to go over there with snow shovels in the winter so we could play."[9] But sometimes you took your life into your hands just by trying to play basketball. Isiah was on the neighborhood court when two players got into an argument over who had the next game. They started pushing and shoving each other.

"Wait here till I get back," one snapped.

Before anyone knew it, he was back toting a gun and opened fire.

"Everybody started running," Thomas said. "I jumped under a car and was hiding. The guy shot him, and I'm laying under the car. When he fell and rolled over, I could see the blood. I can't move, 'cause I'm scared to."[10] Living in K-Town was hazardous to your health.

Even at a fun time, carnival time, there was danger. Isiah and his mother were on the school grounds when suddenly Isiah saw some figures on a rooftop. Members of the Black Souls gang were pointing guns at the rival Vice Lords, who were on the carnival grounds.

At the same time, Isiah's mom spotted them and started shouting, "Get down from there! Get down!"[11]

They did. Isiah's mother was a force in the neighborhood. A frightened Isiah thought, *That bullet could have been meant for me.*

Living in the neighborhood, you could never let your guard down. If you were fortunate enough to be alive, there were other ways your life might be destroyed. Drugs and alcohol were prevalent and had affected Isiah's family. Would Isiah follow the destructive paths of his older brothers? One day, Larry Thomas got a shock. Strutting down the street wearing his expensive suit and hat was his younger brother Isiah. Angry and upset, he took Isiah aside. Larry hated his lifestyle and pleaded with Isiah not to follow in his footsteps.

Larry then started devoting a lot of time to his younger brother, sharpening his skills on the basketball court. He implored Isiah to make it to the NBA, and do it for his brothers who had tried and failed. He was the family's last hope.

The family had a dream. Isiah would be the dream maker.

"Out of all my brothers, he was the one who really saved me," Isiah said of Larry. "At that time in my life, I was lost."[12]

He found himself. But not before he was rejected at the local high school basketball powerhouse. Isiah Thomas, who would be one of the greatest point guards in NBA history, was told by the coach he was too small to play for the school.

Isiah was deeply disappointed. He wanted to play basketball somewhere. That somewhere turned out to be St. Joseph High School in the predominantly white suburb of Westchester. It was a tough commute for Isiah—an hour and a half by bus every morning, counting the three transfers.

Isiah would wake at 5:30 every morning for school. He was reluctant to go outside and face the cold and the howling winds, which are common during Chicago winters.

"I used to feel sorry for him," Mary Thomas said. "I watched him leave and I cried."[13]

Isiah would get on the bus while it was still dark. It was daylight when he got off, but he had to walk an additional two miles before he got to school.

Long bus rides. Long days at school. Long basketball practices.

As a freshman, Isiah struggled academically. Basketball coach Gene Pingatore talked to his new recruit. "You won't be able to play unless you get your academics straightened out."[14] Motivated, Isiah went to summer school. The coach never had to speak to him again about academics. He became an honor-roll student.

Pingatore felt he was the hardest worker on the basketball team, but totally out of control. Isiah took wild shots, throwing the ball up from almost anywhere. Pingatore pulled him out of games when he went crazy. "He would take an outside shot he knew I didn't like, and run to the bench before I yanked him. He knew he was coming out."[15]

By his junior year, Isiah was playing with more restraint. Result: a second-place finish in the state tournament for St. Joseph. When the players returned, they were greeted with a parade. An outsider to the community, Isiah became a local hero.

Isiah was a natural, and it wasn't unusual for him to score 40 points in a game. Yet St. Joseph lost two of its first three games in his senior year. The coach called Isiah into his office. His message: Distribute the ball more. Let others shoot.

He did. St. Joseph's started winning, and didn't lose until an upset on the last shot in the last game of the season.

Dozens of colleges clamored for Isiah's services and offered incentives. The Thomas family had learned the lessons of the streets: Don't owe anything to anyone. They knew there had to be a payback down the road.

And so when Indiana coach Bobby Knight visited, he offered only a good education and fair treatment on the basketball court. That was fine with Mary Thomas. Isiah signed with the Hoosiers. "The one thing that I'm really proud of is the fact that we don't owe anything to anyone," Mary Thomas said.[16]

Knight was tough. He could be demanding and tyrannical, even abusive. But he had won a national championship and was regarded as one of the top college coaches in the country.

When Isiah started playing for Knight, he might have had second thoughts. His relationship with the hot-tempered Indiana coach was often volatile. One day, Knight kicked Isiah out of practice. Two weeks later, he made him team captain. Isiah and Knight basically agreed on basketball philosophy, but as a teenager Isiah sometimes resented Knight's advice on off-the-court matters. It was a roller-coaster ride, with the national championship as the final destination.

Isiah flourished under Knight's system. Knight made compromises in his game plan to suit Isiah's individual talents. "He let me be more creative. In another college system, I would have been stuck in a pattern. I know I would not have developed into as good a college player as I was."[17]

Isiah's family stuck by him. His mother was a familiar figure in the stands, proudly rooting for her son. She was vocal—in her praise and criticism. Once during a big game, Isiah threw a bad pass. He heard his mother's loud voice over the crowd: "What the hell are you doing?"[18]

There were times when Isiah was embarrassed by his family. Some of his brothers were having a difficult time fighting their addictions. They would come to the games and create disturbances. Once during a game, his brother Gregory stood under the backboards shouting continually. Isiah appreciated Knight's treatment of his family. He never made an issue of the problems they were causing.

But Isiah was concerned about his family. The conditions they were living in were deplorable. One time, it really hit home. Isiah came back to K-Town one day to find the gas and electricity shut off, no food in the house, and his mom suffering chest pains. The life-and-death struggles of everyday living in the ghetto were inescapable. Isiah was determined to find a way out through basketball.

All–Big Ten in his first year, All-America in his second, Isiah became one of the most popular players at Indiana.When he walked into lecture halls on mornings following a game, it was not unusual for him to be greeted by a standing ovation.

In the 1980–81 season, Isiah heard more than his share of ovations as the Hoosiers rolled through the season. Going into the NCAA tournament, the Hoosiers were No. 9 in the Associated Press rankings. There would be four grueling games against top-flight competition before the finals. Guess who was still standing when it was time for the championship game?

Indiana faced North Carolina, a team that had crushed them during the season. The Hoosiers found themselves as the underdog, a familiar position for Isiah Thomas.

Isiah's addiction was basketball. When he played, he was usually so focused he did not hear the crowd. He was in his own world when he helped turn the game around against North Carolina with two key steals in the second half. He scored 23 points and was named the tournament's Most Valuable Player as Indiana won its second NCAA title under Knight.

Isiah had an important decision to make. Under an NBA "hardship" rule, players were allowed to leave school before their class graduated. In Isiah's case, hardship was more than a legal term. It was a harsh reality of his life. His family was so poor that his mother very often didn't have enough money for bus fare, and he didn't have any money for haircuts. Three of his brothers were addicted to drugs, and Isiah needed the money to put them into a drug-rehabilitation program. If they didn't get help, he feared, they would die within the year.

Yet he also felt an obligation to graduate. He would be the first in his family to do so, and a role model for other student athletes. Many college basketball players have been seduced by big-money professional contracts. He also knew that a college degree was important, both to himself and his mother.

So they compromised. Isiah signed a contract with the Detroit Pistons, but only after he signed a personal contract with his mother, actually drawn up by lawyers. Isiah wrote in the contract: "I will finish school."[19] After several years as an all-star in the NBA, he fulfilled the promise by getting his degree in criminal justice in 1987.

Isiah was a thirteen-time NBA all-star, a two-time Most Valuable Player in the All-Star Game, and a two-time NBA champion with the Detroit Pistons. Creating something out of the air was one of Isiah's biggest talents. Creating controversies was another.

After a playoff loss to the Boston Celtics, Detroit forward Dennis Rodman said Larry Bird, a future Hall of Famer, was "overrated" because he was white. Thomas agreed. Isiah later said he didn't mean it as a slight against Bird—only that athletes were being stereotyped: whites as "intelligent" and blacks as "athletic." The remark created news, as did the alleged "freezeout" of Michael Jordan in the 1985 All-Star Game. Allegations were made in the media—denied by Thomas—that he and other veterans refused to

Creating something out of the air was one of Isiah's biggest talents. *(AP Wide World)*

pass the ball to the popular rookie because, among other things, they thought he was too arrogant. The allegations appeared to be well founded. Jordan, the NBA rookie of the year that season, scored only seven points—well below his average of 28.2. Then there were allegations of Thomas's call for the trade of a teammate he didn't like. His fight with Pistons teammate Bill Laimbeer wasn't alleged. That, too, created news for the team known as the "Bad Boys."

Thomas admitted he was no angel. "You've got to understand. I'm six foot one. If I was six-nine, I could be 'nice.' "[20]

Things were more settled at home. Thomas had established financial security for his family—a longtime dream. He was happy to give his mother, his main support on the way up the ladder, "peace of mind."

"She didn't have to worry every time the phone rang. She didn't have to wonder if one of her sons was dead or alive. She didn't have to scrape and scuffle and look down to the bottom of her purse for fifty cents to come up with bus fare. One of the greatest gifts I gave her was the opportunity to see her sons and daughters with a chance for life."[21]

Against the odds, the dream maker had come through.

9

BUCK WILLIAMS

Buck Williams was just a rookie in the NBA and hardened veterans were already finding him tough. A battler under the backboards, Williams soon became one of the league's best rebounders. It is a reflection of his life.

Growing up in Rocky Mount, North Carolina, every day was a test of survival.

He brought those survival instincts to a basketball court, where he usually played "hungry." Memories from long ago continually echoed in his mind. . . .

The oppressive North Carolina sun beat down as Betty Williams stooped to pick cotton. Sweat dripped down her arms and forehead. She glanced at a tree where she had placed her son, Charles, on a sheet. It was the only place with shade on that suffocating August day.

Her baby was content sucking from the milk bottle. But danger was ever present. The milk attracted snakes. "They smell the milk and go right down their throats," she said with a shiver.[1]

Blazing a trail to the basket, while teammates look on.
(Portland Trail Blazers)

One of her bags was already bulging with cotton. She had picked a large amount in her morning's work. Still, it was not enough. It was never enough when you were paid only $4 for every hundred pounds. There was barely enough money to put food on the table and clothes on the backs of the five Williams children.

This was the world of Charles "Buck" Williams. Long before he soared over basketball rims, he and his family were just trying to survive in their ghetto neighborhood. Buck's ancestors had been slaves, and that cycle of devastating poverty continued.

It seemed to Buck that people who worked the hardest, picking cotton and tobacco, scrubbing floors sixteen hours a day, made the least amount of money. His father worked long hours on a construction gang, making only ten cents a day. With his own hands, Moses Williams built his family a house—a shack, really, just four rooms with no hot water and no plumbing.

Just a trip to the bathroom was an adventure. The family was forced to use an outhouse. Many a winter morning, Buck would struggle out of bed in his pajamas to be met with an icy blast of air as he crunched through the grass toward the outdoor bathroom.

"At night, I would pray for indoor plumbing," Williams remembered. "It was embarrassing to come home from school, even with my friends, and walk past my house. It was a small little shack that we lived in."[2]

Prayer was a way of life for the Williamses. It

gave them hope. And they weren't afraid of hard work. They never missed a day. There was never much thought about saving money for the future, just about how they were going to make it from one day to the next.

Buck's mother's work ethic in the cotton fields was contagious.

"That's what she had to do to care for her child," said Williams. "And that's the strength I came from. Regardless of your situation, you still can somehow forge ahead and try to find a way to survive. Those were the survival instincts that not only my mother had, but I had as well."[3]

His parents weren't Buck's only role models. He admired Jack Johnson, the great black boxer of the twenties, "because he never let anyone define his existence. He was his own man, and he wasn't going to let America or anyone else tell him his place in society."[4] He also loved Kareem Abdul-Jabbar, the great basketball star of the Los Angeles Lakers.

Poverty. It can be an ugly word filled with despair and hopelessness. For many Americans, it is a way of life. Few of them ever rise above it. Buck Williams was determined to be an exception.

Buck got his first job. He was the baby of the family and only twelve years old when he started working. The thought of making fifty cents an hour made the hard work in the warehouse stacking shelf after shelf with candy more bearable. He knew just what he was going to buy with his first paycheck—an egg beater! His mother worked so hard that Buck wanted her to have things she couldn't afford. He kept the job throughout high school, and Betty Williams used the egg beater for many years.

Buck was about to discover basketball—or was it the other way around?

Buck was playing football in junior high. He hadn't thought much about basketball until a friend asked him to join the team. "I started playing basketball, and I fell in love with it."[5]

And Reggie Henderson fell in love with Williams. The coach of the Rocky Mount High School team, Henderson urged Williams to develop his talents in the tough Sonny Hill summer league in Philadelphia.

Williams didn't play much his first summer, but his second summer was great. He led the highly regarded summer league in rebounding. "At that point, I just realized that these are the best players in the country and if I can play with these players, I can play with anyone."[6]

A player who had stumbled upon basketball in junior high school suddenly had become a terror on the court in high school. Need a rebound? Williams got it. Need a winning basket? No sweat.

"His work ethic is exemplary," Henderson said. "His job on my team was to be a rebounder, and so he thought that every ball that went off the glass, that was his. Every shot that was taken, he would try to get into a rebound position. That was his job. He worked at it and worked at it."[7]

Rebounding was a simple process for Buck.

"I just know where the ball is going," he ex-

A study in concentration: Buck Williams. *(Portland Trail Blazers)*

plained. "A lot of times, I can head-fake my man one way and go the other for the ball."[8]

Williams led Rocky Mount to the state championship and was named the tournament's Most

Valuable Player. He finished his high school career with more than 1,000 rebounds and 1,000 points. A high school All-America, he was heavily recruited. He was expected to go to North Carolina, the premier state school. He did the unexpected—he went to Maryland instead.

"I didn't play organized basketball until the ninth grade, so it was critical to play more basketball," Williams said. "North Carolina had three or four players in my position. Maryland had only one power forward, and that gave me hope of playing some big minutes."[9]

Buck had his dreams. He dreamed of being an NBA star. He dreamed of a beautiful home for his family, with hot water and indoor plumbing. It wasn't until he was in tenth grade that the family had hot water for the first time. He wanted to do so much for his mother and father, who had always supported him. Basketball was the answer—a way to get the American Dream.

When Williams drove onto the University of Maryland campus he was hard to miss. While most students were driving the family car, Buck drove into town in a souped-up '72 Chevelle. The car was a sight to see: blue, with thick, wide stripes running from the hood to the back, and a CB antenna jutting out of the trunk.

Buck was fascinated by hot-rod cars and spent hours working on them—much to the amusement of his teammates. Like his father, Williams could express himself by working with his hands.

Even though he was driving a Chevelle around the campus, he was a Cadillac on the court for the Maryland Terps. As a freshman, he led the Atlantic Coast Conference in rebounding and was named the league's Rookie of the Year.

"He would not be intimidated by anybody," teammate Greg Manning remembered. "He was just physically strong. He was relentless on the boards. He was an animal. He'd go get the offensive rebound and get it back out. He'd get the defensive boards. He'd get the fast break started."[10]

Williams did his share of the scoring at Maryland, but it was in the less glamorous parts of the game that he really stood out.

Instead of the high-profile jobs of shooters and ball handlers, Williams was content to do the basics of basketball: rebound, play interior defense, set picks for teammates. It was the family work ethic translated to a basketball court. "He did a lot of things that other guys didn't want to do," Manning said. "If you get beat out up top, he helps you inside. You just yell, 'Hey, Buck . . .' It got to be a habit with me."[11]

Buck showed his versatility at Maryland. He started out as a forward, then switched to center in his sophomore year. As a 6-foot-8, 215-pound center, he usually played against much taller opponents, such as Virginia's 7-foot-4 Ralph Sampson. Sampson said Williams was the toughest player who guarded him.

Tough player, then a tough decision.

Buck had spent an agonizing night, and a midnight deadline was looming. He was a religious person with high moral standards. Was he about to let everybody down?

"I was sure that the people at Maryland would hate me," Williams said. "I felt indebted to them."[12]

Buck had to decide whether or not to declare "hardship" to join the NBA. Buck never made a spontaneous decision. He thought it out one step at a time. "It's like building a model car. If you hurry through it, you might miss some part. And then it really wouldn't be what you wanted."[13]

But this decision was giving him difficulty. He thought of all the people who went hardship and didn't succeed. Surprisingly, people like Magic Johnson and Adrian Dantley never entered his mind. And he thought of all the others who might follow his example and fail.

"Other players will see me and think they can do it, too. Sometimes, a team will pick a guy and never use him."[14]

Yet he knew what he could do for his family with pro money, and the timing was right. He would be one of the highest-drafted players. He made his decision. The New Jersey Nets picked him as No. 3 in the 1981 draft, and he signed a contract for $450,000 a season.

He had realized one dream. Now he could realize another. Before he bought anything for himself, he bought his mom and dad a new home. "That has probably given me more joy than anything as an adult," he says. It was the best day in his life. The shack he grew up in, which had stood for twenty-six years, was replaced. His mom was thrilled with the "mansion—four bedrooms, three bathrooms, and all them showers."[15]

Once again, Williams was the pillar of a basketball team. He was a 1,000-rebound man in his first year in the NBA and named the league's Rookie of the Year. He made a science out of rebounding.

"You have to hold your ground, get the spot you want, and not give it up for the world. You have to anticipate and get the jump on them; if you wait, there's no way you're going to stop them from getting to the goal. If they push you too far in, you might as well not be there."[16]

Position was everything in life—at least in the NBA. One play against the Phoenix Suns typified Buck's rookie season.

The Nets were winning by two points with 1:23 left. After a missed shot, Williams leaped for the offensive rebound. He locked it in with his strong, limber hands. Fouled on his follow-up shot, he sank two free throws to clinch the victory for the Nets.

Williams loved the challenge of offensive rebounding.

"It means I beat that defense all alone. I crushed what they wanted to do. They can't run because I got the ball."[17]

Williams wasn't always proud of everything he did.

The Nets were playing New York in Buck's rookie year. During a battle under the backboard, Williams suddenly found himself gripped in a fierce headlock by former teammate Maurice Lucas. Williams fired a roundhouse punch to Lucas's jaw.

"I just lost all control," Williams remembered. "It was a rookie thing to do . . . but I had to let him know that I wasn't going to let him push me around. Sometimes you can get pushed right out of the league."[18]

Pushing around the Nets as a team was easier. They were being pushed around by everyone in the league, losing game after game. For the first time in his career, Williams played for a losing team. Day after day. Game after game. He was in a rut.

"It was very difficult losing those games. Sometimes you lose so many, you begin to wonder if you're a loser."[19]

But Williams refused to act like a loser. Under those trying circumstances, he came to work every day and gave everything he had. "As long as I could live with my effort, I was satisfied." For eight years, he gave his all for a team that was going nowhere. He played every day as if it were the first day. "It was really character-building for me," he emphasized. "There's no question that New Jersey conditioned me, made me a better player. Facing unbelievable odds and dealing with it can often lead to a consistency of work ethic."[20]

During this time, he went back to school to set a good example for his children and protect his future. Buck joked, "I'm making a million a year and I have homework."[21] He got his degree in business administration in 1988.

About the same time, Williams did another kind of study. He had been troubled by questions concerning his family background. He traced his mother's family tree back to 1800. It made Buck angry going through slave owners' records. One of his ancestors was listed along with the livestock at a value of $150. He saw a similarity to his own circumstances. Even though he was extremely well paid, he was "owned" as a basketball player and could be either traded or sold to another team at the whim of management. "Here I was treated just like that," Williams said in reference to his slave ancestors.[22]

Even more oppressive, although he accepted it, was the bondage he felt as a member of the struggling Nets. But it didn't affect his work ethic.

"I always wanted to try to work very hard and let the public know that even though I was in a losing situation, I was working hard. And what happened was they really appreciated my work ethic and how I pretty much endured losing and showed character."[23]

Williams appeared to be doomed to finish out his career in New Jersey. He was the Nets' most popular player. Fans identified with his work ethic. But the Nets finally traded him to the Portland Trail Blazers. At first, he had mixed feelings about leaving New Jersey, but Portland became a good fit.

The Trail Blazers were perennial playoff failures. They had a reputation for selfish play. They needed the unselfish Williams to show them the way. He did. Williams blazed the way for the Trail Blazers. They found themselves in the NBA finals for the first time since 1977—not once, but two times in a three-year period. Williams always felt like a winner, but now he was actually with a winning team.

Not even losses in the NBA finals could diminish Portland's accomplishments, or what Williams had meant to the Trail Blazers. Detroit's Isiah Thomas was asked the difference between the 1988–89 and 1989–90 Trailblazers. "Buck Williams," was the answer.

Few players were more respected thanWilliams. One opposing coach made up a videotape of Buck's greatest moments on the court as an instructional tool for young forwards. Williams was a model of consistency and durability—he missed only five games in his first five years in Portland. He had missed only twenty-one with the Nets. He marked his sixteenth season in the NBA playing for the New York Knicks during 1996–97.

In spite of his success, he has never forgotten his roots. There were times his mom would talk about the family struggle in dealing with poverty. She'd talk about it at the drop of a hat, and in the company of virtual strangers. Many times Buck would be embarrassed. He'd think, *Mom, they don't need to know that.*

"So many African-Americans are hesitant to talk about the struggle of being poor. But I'm convinced dealing with it gives you strength," Buck says.[24]

The struggles of his family and his ancestors are ever present in his mind. "Situations are either going to make you or break you. And those situations made my family a very strong unit."[25]

He has brought the American Dream to himself and his family. He now flies jets over the same land that once held him in the grip of poverty. "Seeing sunsets, seeing coastlines. You know what's amazing? Sometimes I'll sit there in a plane and just sort of reflect back on my hometown, and I just can't believe it. I was brought up in poverty and [was] sort of hopeless at a certain point. And here I am now, flying a Cessna with the whole world open for me."[26]

10

HOT ROD WILLIAMS

Hot Rod Williams had to come home sometime. The police were waiting. Soon the nightmare would begin.

A model citizen and NBA standout today, Williams was then fighting for his reputation and his life. It was 1985, and Hot Rod was a senior at Tulane University.

Barbara Colar, his mother, was shocked when the police came to her door. They had an arrest warrant for Hot Rod. They searched the house. Hot Rod was equally shocked when he came home to find the police waiting for him.

What did I do? he wanted to know. *I didn't do nothing.*

He was read his rights. The charge: bank robbery.

They whisked him out of the house and took him to the local police station to be fingerprinted. Then they drove him to New Orleans.

I didn't do nothing. . . .

In New Orleans, he heard the truth. He was actually being charged with sports bribery for alleg-

---

Hot Rod gave Tulane life with his shooting ability. (*Tulane University*)

edly "shaving" points in three basketball games for Tulane. The practice of point shaving is a sad part of basketball history, one that surfaces every so often to give the sport a black eye.

"Bribery? What is bribery?" Williams asked authorities. "Someone explain to me what I did."[1]

One of the most notorious episodes in the college game occurred in the 1950–51 season. Players on the City College of New York team were found to be "shaving points"—holding down the score in certain games to favor the betting point spread for gamblers. Incredibly, CCNY managed to beat Bradley for the national championship—not once, but twice, in the NCAA and NIT finals—despite many players purposely not playing their best.

Now, thirty-four years later, a group of Tulane University players and students were being accused of a similar scheme. John "Hot Rod" Williams and Jon Johnson were the two most prominent of the players involved.

What followed was fifteen months of the darkest time in Williams's life. He faced the possibility of seventeen years in prison and the loss of a promising basketball career, not to mention a crushing blow to his family life. He and his high school sweetheart, Karen Hardy, had a son, John Jr.

His mother, Barbara Colar, was devastated. John had been an orphan, less than a year old, when she had taken him in and raised him as her own. Their bond was unbreakable.

John Williams was born in Sorrento, Louisiana,

a poor, rural community about fifty miles from New Orleans that had once served as a railroad stop between New Orleans and Baton Rouge. The population was less than a thousand. It was so hot in the summertime, it was said you could cook eggs on the sidewalk.

Williams's biological mother died when he was seven months old. His father walked out, leaving him with his maternal grandfather, Felton Williams. But the man could hardly care for his grandson—he was seventy-eight years old and blind.

Colar stepped in. As a neighbor, she had heard the baby's pitiful cries from the front porch of the dilapidated row house. She brought him home. "The lady fit me into her family just like I was her own," Williams said.[2]

Williams said he never knew he was adopted until he was seven years old. When Colar told him, he protested.

"No, you my real mama!" he blurted out between sobs, not wanting to believe anything else.[3] Truly, Colar had treated John Williams no differently than she had her other three children. And he had needed special care, due to an asthmatic condition that often troubled him while he was at play.

It was always the same: Hot Rod would be out playing with other kids, and suddenly the asthma would strike. His chest tightened, as though someone were pulling a belt around him. Gasping, he struggled to fill his lungs with air. Would he ever be able to breathe normally again?

"My mother would have to rush me to the hospital," Williams remembered. "At the time, we had to go to a charity hospital. When you go to a charity hospital, you have to wait in line like everybody else. It's not like a paid hospital, where they take you right in. We sat in that hospital many nights where people would just forget we were out there. By the time they would come out to get us, I'd tell my mama, 'You can take me home, it's gone away.' "[4]

Doctors told Williams he could not play basketball. He refused to accept that. "I told my mom, 'I'm going to play ball,' because that's what I wanted to do. All my friends were doing it."[5] Playing ball, Williams was always known as Hot Rod. Colar had given him the nickname when he was a little boy racing around the floor making grinding sounds.

Home to the Colars was a little trailer set up in a small cluster of trailers outside Sorrento. Tom Green, an assistant coach who helped recruit Hot Rod for Tulane University, remembered the ride to the Colars' place.

"It was very much rural. You jump off Highway Ten, go by a couple of service stations. The side road that went up to this little trailer area, before you got to town, was maybe four or five miles away." There were six or eight trailers clustered in an area about the size of a small town block. "It was very small. You wouldn't even qualify it as a trailer park."[6]

Conditions were already crowded in the trailer when Hot Rod joined the family. "What they had inside the house was very clean," Green said, "but they didn't have a whole lot."

There were spiritual riches there. "It was a happy place. There were always kids going and coming, everybody speaking and everybody smiling."[7]

And near the trailer was The Court, where Hot Rod got his early basketball experience. There were no basketball courts in town. "When I was growing up, the town couldn't afford a basketball court," Williams said. So Hot Rod and his friends made their own right there in their trailer park. "We used to take a bicycle rim and take the spokes out and hang it on a piece of board and make a goal."[8]

The makeshift dirt court was uneven and bumpy. "With us running and jumping on it so much, the ground would give. You couldn't dribble the ball."[9] Williams learned how to shoot without putting the ball on the ground.

The uneven ground wasn't the only drawback.

"When you got through playing and you had a pair of white socks on, you had to throw them away because they weren't anything but sand socks, because the sand and the sweat mixed together would turn them into mud," Williams said.[10]

Williams wanted to play high school ball, but he had a problem. He couldn't get a ride home from practice. Tommy Wall, the coach at St. Amant High School, made sure he had a ride home in his junior year—at 6 feet 5, Williams was the tallest student in school, and Wall wanted him on the team in the worst way. By that time, Williams was focused and very mature. "Sometimes teams tried to intimidate him, saying things about his family. He managed to shut all that out," Wall said.

Williams was a welcome addition to the St. Amant team.

"We went nine and twenty-four without him, and then fifty-eight and sixteen the next two seasons," Wall said.[11]

As a senior, Williams led his team to the quarterfinals of the state tournament. That season, Williams was also named Most Valuable Player in a Louisiana high school all-star game featuring future NBA players Joe Dumars and Karl Malone.

Williams credited his high school coach with his development, both on and off the court. "Tommy Wall was a great friend of mine. He was like a father to me."[12] Williams's relationship with Wall was important to him. He needed an older man's advice and support as he struggled through the teenage years. Williams remembered meeting his natural father when he was about eleven or twelve years old. The meeting didn't last very long. "He tried to give me five dollars, and I gave it back," Williams recalled. "I wasn't really mad, but five dollars wasn't what I wanted."[13]

Even though he had become a prominent basketball player, Williams was painfully shy in high school. He walked around "with my head down to the ground. My teachers would ask me, 'Why you never say anything?' But that was just my way."[14] His basketball prominence did give him more confidence with girls, though. As a junior he met Karen Hardy, whom he dated and eventually married.

Despite his high school exploits in basketball, Williams was not heavily recruited by colleges. "He was real skinny and weak," remembered Ned Fowler, then coach at Tulane. "He weighed maybe 190 pounds. He was not a good shooter fundamentally. There were questions as to whether he'd be a good major-college player."[15] The raw talent was there. The problem was, Williams never really had the time to develop it. He had to get jobs wherever he could to help support his family.

But Tulane took a gamble and gave Williams a basketball scholarship. They knew Williams was a diamond in the rough. He needed the edges smoothed out, and he needed to bulk up. The day he committed to Tulane, Assistant Coach Kirk Saulny told Fowler: "If this kid works on weights and gets stronger, he can play in the NBA."[16]

Even though he didn't have a basketball body, Hot Rod had a basketball mind.

"We called different plays almost every time," Saulny said. "John probably could have told you what every player on the team does on every play. He had a clinical-type mind for basketball."[17]

It isn't often a player steps right in and starts as a freshman in a major college basketball program, particularly a player with only two years of high school experience. Williams did it with an exclamation point. He was named Rookie of the Year in the Metro Seven Conference. When his performance dropped off as a sophomore, Williams's pride was hurt.

This is not going to happen to me again.

Williams rededicated himself. He worked harder in the weight room and on his shooting in the off-season. Result: Metro Conference Player of the Year as a junior. Everything was going smoothly.

But there was trouble ahead.

It started when Hot Rod's trailer burned to the ground.

"There was nothing left but rubble," Saulny said. "For people living in a trailer, without much to begin with, it was a devastating situation."[18]

One businessman let the family move into a house he was renovating. They could stay there for a couple of months. Although NCAA regulations prohibited Tulane from offering any financial assistance, Fowler gave Williams $100 here and there. NCAA regulations be damned, he said.

"I gave John money because he had a baby, his house burned down, and he was penniless," Fowler said. "How can I look a boy in the face without a dime in his pocket and say, 'I'm sorry, but I can't help you'? In my case, I did the right thing and it turned out wrong."[19]

Fowler would get into trouble for his Good Samaritan deed. And Williams was about to get into trouble for his alleged misdeeds.

In the world of sports gambling, it doesn't matter if you win or lose, but whether you cover the spread. Each game has a betting line, judged on the strengths and weaknesses of the teams. For instance, if you bet on the stronger team to win, you have to "give" points—that is, your team not only has to win, but must win by a certain number of points. If you bet on the weaker team, you "take" points. Your team can lose, but you can still win the bet if it stays within the point spread.

Williams and four other players were accused of taking money from gamblers to shave points. Three other students were also involved.

Jon Johnson, testifying under immunity, admitted his guilt. Some of the other key witnesses were also given immunity or pleaded guilty to lesser charges for their testimony.

Williams did not.

"He [Johnson] can say what he wants and you can write what you want. I can't control that," Williams told reporters. "But I know what happened. I'll look anyone in the eye and say I didn't do it, because that's the truth."[20]

There had been bad blood between Williams and Johnson. Williams was getting most of the publicity for the team's performance, and he felt Johnson was jealous. In Williams's junior year, the two had a huge fight and had to be forcibly pulled apart.

It was hard to imagine Williams doing any less than his best in the games involved in the alleged point shaving. Against Southern Mississippi, Williams made all of his six shots in the second half. Against Memphis State, he scored 10 of his 14 points after intermission.

Not everyone thought Williams was guilty. Harry Weltman, who was the general manager of the Cleveland Cavaliers at the time, had done some investigating on his own. He was convinced Williams was innocent and that he would be exonerated. "Really, the D.A. and the media did a number on him. The whole thing was reprehensible," Weltman said.[21]

Despite warnings from the NBA, the Cavaliers made Williams a second-round pick in the draft. Williams was a risk, but one that Weltman didn't mind taking. His team had just come off a losing season, and Williams could really help the Cavaliers—if he ever got to play.

"I knew I could make that team," said Williams after practicing with the Cavaliers.[22]

But first there was a trial and a chance he could wind up in jail. He was at the center of a firestorm that sparked unwanted national headlines at Tulane. Eventually, Fowler and his staff would step down and the basketball program would be disbanded.

A mistrial was declared in Williams's case: The district attorney had withheld evidence in his favor.

Williams went to trial for a second time. The NBA declared him ineligible for the 1985–86 season. The most Williams could do was practice with players who were on the injured list. He kept himself in game shape by playing in the upstart United States Basketball League. It also helped take his mind off his problems.

At the second trial, Williams was counting on a favorable verdict.

Soaring for a rebound. *(Phoenix Suns)*

"I had a lot of stress on me, but I didn't go crazy," he said. "I knew I was going to play in the NBA."

How?

"I knew I didn't do anything wrong."[23]

The jury thought so, too. After two trials and fifteen agonizing months of mental torture and strain, Hot Rod Williams was found innocent by a jury that deliberated less than three hours.

That chapter of his life finally closed, Williams could now join the NBA. The 6-foot-11, 245-pound Williams became an invaluable player for the Cavaliers—first as a "sixth man" off the bench and then as a starter, where he played solidly in two positions—forward and center. In his first season, he made the NBA's All-Rookie team. For many years, he has been one of the league's most consistent performers. Regarded as a basketball "genius" for his innate ability to understand the game, he always seemed to be there when his team needed a spark on offense or defense.

Finally, his big payoff came. In 1990, the Cavaliers handed him a five-year contract worth $26.5 million. At that time, it was the second-highest salary for a team player in any sport in America.

With his financial worries over, he was able to make some paybacks. He donated a basketball court to his community and kept a promise he once made to Barbara Colar to provide her with a better life. He felt it was the least he could do; she had raised him and stood by him through good and bad times.

Now a father of three, Williams sums up his life "like climbing a set of steps to a house."

"I've had a couple of them steps break on me, and I've fallen down, been delayed, but I've never given up on anything," said Williams, who was traded to the Phoenix Suns in 1995. "If you quit once, you're beaten forever."[24]

Source Notes

Chapter 1
Mahmoud Abdul-Rauf

1. *Sports Illustrated,* November 15, 1993
2. *The Sporting News,* February 20, 1989
3. *The Sporting News,* February 20, 1989
4. Author's interview
5. Author's interview
6. *Sports Illustrated,* November 15, 1993
7. *Seattle Post-Intelligencer,* April 30, 1994
8. *The Sporting News,* February 14, 1994
9. *The Main Event,* Fall 1990
10. Author's interview
11. *Sports Illustrated,* February 20, 1989
12. *Seattle Post-Intelligencer,* April 30, 1994
13. *Seattle Post-Intelligencer,* April 30, 1994
14. *The Sporting News,* February 14, 1994
15. *The Sporting News,* February 14, 1994
16. *The Sporting News,* November 15, 1993
17. *The Sporting News,* February 14, 1994
18. *Seattle Post-Intelligencer,* April 30, 1994

Chapter 2
Muggsy Bogues

1. Author's interview
2. Author's interview
3. *New York Times,* February 27, 1995
4. *New York Times,* February 27, 1995
5. *New York Times,* February 27, 1995
6. Author's interview
7. *Greensboro* (N.C.) *News & Record,* February 1, 1987
8. Author's interview

9. Author's interview
10. Author's interview
11. *Sports Illustrated,* February 16, 1987
12. *The Olympian,* March 1987
13. *The Olympian,* March 1987
14. *Sports Illustrated,* February 16, 1987
15. *The Olympian,* March 1987
16. *New York Times,* February 27, 1995
17. *New York Times,* February 27, 1996
18. *The Sporting News,* 1994–95 Pro Basketball Yearbook
19. *The Sporting News,* 1994–95 Pro Basketball Yearbook
20. *New York Times,* February 27, 1995

Chapter 3
Bobby Hurley

1. *Sports Illustrated,* May 23, 1994
2. *Reader's Digest,* December 1995
3. *Sports Illustrated,* November 23, 1992
4. *Sports Illustrated,* November 23, 1992
5. *Esquire,* March 1993
6. *Esquire,* March 1993
7. *Sports Illustrated,* November 23, 1992
8. *Sports Illustrated,* May 23, 1994
9. Author's interview
10. Author's interview
11. *Sports Illustrated,* May 23, 1994
12. *People,* November 14, 1994
13. Author's interview
14. *People,* November 14, 1994
15. *People,* November 14, 1994
16. *Reader's Digest,* December 1995
17. Author's interview
18. Author's interview

Chapter 4
John Lucas

1. *Boston Globe,* February 13, 1993
2. *Parade* magazine, May 16, 1993

3. *Parade* magazine, May 16, 1993
4. Author's interview
5. *The Sporting News,* March 29, 1993
6. *Parade* magazine, May 16, 1993
7. Author's interview
8. *Parade* magazine, May 16, 1993
9. *The Sporting News,* January 18, 1993
10. *Chicago Sun-Times,* January 24, 1993
11. *Ebony,* June 1993
12. *Ebony,* June 1993
13. *Boston Globe,* February 13, 1993
14. *The Sporting News,* March 29, 1993
15. *Ebony,* June 1993
16. *Parade* magazine, May 16, 1993
17. *Beckett Basketball,* May 1993
18. *The Sporting News,* March 29, 1993
19. *Sports Illustrated,* January 11, 1993
20. *The Sporting News,* March 29, 1993

Chapter 5
Reggie Miller

1. Associated Press, May 7, 1995
2. *New Brunswick* (N.J.) *Home News,* May 8, 1995
3. *Indianapolis Monthly,* August 1994
4. *The Sporting News,* December 26, 1994
5. *The Sporting News,* December 26, 1994
6. *The Sporting News,* December 26, 1994
7. *Los Angeles Times,* March 2, 1986
8. *Indianapolis Monthly,* August 1994
9. *Sports Illustrated,* November 7, 1994
10. *Indianapolis News,* May 24, 1994
11. *The Sporting News,* December 26, 1994
12. *The Sporting News,* December 26, 1994
13. Author's interview
14. *The Sporting News,* December 26, 1994
15. *The Sporting News,* December 26, 1994
16. Author's interview

17. Author's interview
18. Author's interview
19. *Los Angeles Times,* March 2, 1996
20. *Pasadena Star-News,* March 2, 1986
21. *Sports Illustrated,* November 7, 1994
22. *Sports Illustrated,* November 7, 1994
23. *The Sporting News,* December 26, 1994
24. *Sports Illustrated,* November 7, 1994
25. *Sports Illustrated,* November 7, 1994
26. *The Sporting News,* December 26, 1994
27. *Indianapolis Monthly,* August 1994
28. *The Sporting News,* December 26, 1994

Chapter 6
Hakeem Olajuwon

1. Author's interview
2. Author's interview
3. Author's interview
4. Author's interview
5. *Sport,* April 1988
6. *The Sporting News,* 1983–84 Basketball Yearbook
7. *Chicago Tribune,* May 22, 1986
8. *Houston Post,* January 8, 1984
9. *Sport,* April 1988
10. *The Sporting News,* 1983–84 Basketball Yearbook
11. *Houston Chronicle,* June 15, 1994
12. *Chicago Tribune,* May 22, 1986
13. *New York Times,* April 4, 1983
14. Author's interview
15. *Sports Illustrated,* November 28, 1983
16. *Sports Illustrated,* November 28, 1983
17. *Sports Illustrated,* November 28, 1983
18. Author's interview
19. Author's interview
20. Author's interview
21. Author's interview
22. *Boston Herald,* June 1, 1986

23. Author's interview
24. Author's interview
25. *Houston Post,* November 1983
26. *New York Times,* April 4, 1984
27. *Esquire,* February 1994

Chapter 7
John Starks

1. *Sport,* February 1994
2. *Inside Sports,* November 1993
3. *New York* magazine, April 12, 1993
4. *Inside Sports,* November 1993
5. *Hoop,* January 1995
6. *Hoop,* January 1995/*New York* magazine, April 12, 1993
7. *New York* magazine, April 12, 1993
8. *New York,* April 12, 1993
9. *St. Louis Post-Dispatch,* February 21, 1988
10. *St. Louis Post-Dispatch,* February 21, 1988
11. *Sport,* October 1993
12. *Daily Oklahoman,* November 9, 1988
13. *St. Louis Post-Dispatch,* February 21, 1988
14. Author's interview
15. Author's interview
16. *New York* magazine, April 12, 1993
17. *New York Times,* February 7, 1994
18. New York *Daily News,* January 5, 1992
19. *New York* magazine, April 12, 1993
20. *Sport,* October 1993
21. *Sport,* February 1994

Chapter 8
Isiah Thomas

1. *Sports Illustrated,* March 20, 1995/January 19, 1987
2. *Sports Illustrated,* March 20, 1995
3. *Sports Illustrated,* January 19, 1987
4. *Toronto Sunday Sun,* May 29, 1994

5. *Sports Illustrated,* January 19, 1987
6. *Sports Illustrated,* January 19, 1987
7. *Sports Illustrated,* January 19, 1987
8. *New York Times,* April 27, 1981
9. *Sports Illustrated,* January 19, 1987
10. *GQ,* February 1988
11. *Sports Illustrated,* March 20, 1995
12. *Sports Illustrated,* January 19, 1987
13. *Sports Illustrated,* January 19, 1987
14. Author's interview
15. Author's interview
16. Author's interview
17. *Sports Illustrated,* March 20, 1995
18. *Sports Illustrated,* March 20, 1995
19. *Sports Illustrated,* March 20, 1993
20. *Sport,* June 1992
21. *Sports Illustrated,* March 20, 1995

Chapter 9
Buck Williams

1. *Sports Illustrated,* January 15, 1990
2. *Sports Illustrated,* January 15, 1990
3. Author's interview
4. Author's interview
5. Author's interview
6. Author's interview
7. Author's interview
8. *Sports Illustrated,* February 1, 1982
9. Author's interview
10. Author's interview
11. Author's interview
12. *Sports Illustrated,* February 1, 1982
13. *Sports Illustrated,* February 1, 1982
14. *Sports Illustrated,* February 1, 1982
15. *Washington Post,* June 10, 1982
16. *Sport,* February 1986
17. *Sport,* February 1986

18. *Sports Illustrated,* February 1, 1982
19. Author's interview
20. Author's interview/*Washington Post,* June 10, 1992
21. *Sports Illustrated,* January 15, 1990
22. *Sports Illustrated,* January 15, 1990
23. Author's interview
24. *Washington Post,* June 10, 1992
25. Author's interview
26. Author's interview

Chapter 10
Hot Rod Williams

1. *Sport,* February 1988
2. Cleveland Cavaliers interview
3. *Sport,* February 1988
4. Cleveland Cavaliers interview
5. Cleveland Cavaliers interview
6. Author's interview
7. Author's interview
8. Cleveland Cavaliers interview
9. Cleveland Cavaliers interview
10. Cleveland Cavaliers interview
11. *Sport,* February 1988
12. *Sport,* February 1988
13. *Sport,* February 1988
14. *Sport,* February 1988
15. *Sport,* February 1988
16. Author's interview
17. Author's interview
18. Author's interview
19. *Sports Illustrated,* April 22, 1985
20. *Sport,* February 1988
21. *Sport,* February 1988
22. *Sport,* February 1988
23. *Sport,* February 1988
24. Cleveland *Plain Dealer,* August 5, 1990

Index

Abdul-Jabbar, Kareem, 111
Abdul-Rauf, Mahmoud, 1–13
All-Star Game, 105–7
Anthony, Greg, 54
Associated Press All-America, 7
Atlantic Coast Conference (ACC), 20, 24, 114–15
Awards, honors
  M. Abdul-Rauf, 6, 7, 12
  M. Bogues, 19, 20, 26–27
  J. Lucas, 43
  R. Miller, 61
  H. Olajuwon, 77, 80
  I. Thomas, 103–4, 105
  B. Williams, 113–14, 115, 117
  H. R. Williams, 128, 130, 134

Baltimore, Md., 16
Barkley, Charles, 78
Batham, Mike, 34
Battle of the Giants, 80
Battle of the Superstar Centers, 68
Biancani, Al, 39, 93
Bird, Larry, 105
Blaisdell, William, 35, 36
Bogues, Anthony, 18
Bogues, Elaine, 17
Bogues, Richard, 17, 27
Bogues, Tyrone (Muggsy), 15–27
Bossett, A. Joyce, 48
Boston Celtics, 27, 105
Bree, Mike, 58–59
Bristow, Allan, 26
Brown, Dale, 6, 8, 9
Brown, Larry, 54, 91

Camden High School, 15, 19
Carse, Craig, 7
Cedar Rapids (Iowa) Silver Bullets, 91–92
Charlotte Hornets, 26–27
City College of New York, 124
Cleveland Cavaliers, 132–34

Colar, Barbara, 123, 124, 125–26, 134
College players turning pro
  M. Abdul-Rauf, 9–10
  M. Bogues, 25–26
  B. Hurley, 33–34
  J. Lucas, 44–45
  H. Olajuwon, 78
  I. Thomas, 104–5
  B. Williams, 115–16
Competitiveness
  M. Abdul-Rauf, 7
  J. Lucas, 43
  R. Miller, 59
Continental Basketball Association (CBA), 91–92, 93
Contracts
  B. Hurley, 33
  B. Williams, 116
  H. R. Williams, 134

Daley, Richard, 98
Dallas Mavericks, 41
Daniels, Mel, 25
Dantley, Adrian, 116
Dawkins, Johnny, 22–24
de la Tourette, Gilles, 2
Denver Nuggets, 1, 10–12
Detroit Pistons, 92, 105, 107
"Dream Team" (first), 78
"Dream Team III," 64
Drexler, Clyde, 77
Driesell, Lefty, 44
Drugs/alcohol, 101, 103, 104–5
  J. Lucas, 41, 44–49
Duke University (Blue Devils), 22–24, 32–33
Dumars, Joe, 128
Dunbar High School, 16, 18

Elmore, Len, 43
Erving, Julius, 3
Ewing, Patrick, 54, 68, 78, 80, 93
Expansion draft, 26

Family(ies)
  see Home and family
Fans, 9, 64, 119
Final Four, 33
Fonde Recreation Center (Houston),
  76
Fowler, Ned, 129, 130, 132

Gerould, Gary, 35–36
Ghetto neighborhood(s), 103
  M. Bogues, 16–17
  I. Thomas, 95–96, 99–100
  B. Williams, 110
Golden State Warriors, 91
Green, Tom, 126–27
Gulfport High School, 4

Hamilton, Leonard, 88–89, 90
Hardy, Karen, 124, 129
Harlem City Tournament, 19
Harper, Derek, 62
Harter, Dick, 26
Hazzard, Walt, 59–60
Height
  H. Olajuwon, 68, 69–70
  I. Thomas, 107
Height, lack of
  M. Bogues, 15–16, 17, 18, 19, 25,
  26
Henderson, Reggie, 112
Hillside High School, 42
Home and family
  M. Bogues, 17
  J. Lucas, 42, 45–46
  R. Miller, 55, 56
  H. Olajuwon, 70, 72, 78
  J. Starks, 85–86
  I. Thomas, 95–97, 100, 103, 107
  B. Williams, 110–12, 114, 116,
    118–19, 120–21
  H. R. Williams, 124–27, 230
Houston Rockets, 44–47, 48, 78,
  80–81
Hurley, Bob, Sr., 30–32, 35, 37
Hurley, Bobby, 29–39
Hurley, Chris, 30, 35
Hurley, Danny, 31

Indiana Pacers, 25, 53–54, 62
Indiana University (Hoosiers),
  102–4

Islam, 12–13
Issel, Dan, 12

Jackson, Chris
  see Abdul-Rauf, Mahmoud
Jackson, Jacqueline, 5–6
Jenkins, Bert, 4
Jenkins, Lil, 6
Jersey Shore Summer League, 37
John Lucas Aftercare Treatment
  and Recovery Center, 48
Johnson, Jack, 111
Johnson, Jon, 124, 131
Johnson, Magic, 116
Jordan, Michael, 78, 105–7
Jump shooting
  R. Miller, 57, 62
  J. Starks, 83

K-Town (Chicago), 95, 99–100, 103
Knight, Bobby, 102–3, 104
Krzyzewski, Mike, 32

Lagos, Nigeria, 70
Laimbeer, Bill, 107
Lewis, Guy, 67–68, 75–77, 78
Lewis, Reggie, 18, 27
Lord, Willie, 97
Los Angeles Clippers, 30, 34
Louisiana State University, 6–9, 10
Lucas, Debbie, 45, 46–47
Lucas, John, 41–51
Lucas, John, Sr., 42
Lucas, Maurice, 117–18
Lucas, Tarvia, 45–46

McCombs, Red, 41, 42
McGuire, Al, 24
McMillen, Tom, 43, 44
McNeal, Marty, 34
Mackey, Kevin, 48
Madison Square Garden, 53, 61
Malone, Karl, 128
Malone, Moses, 26, 76
Manning, Greg, 115
Maravich, "Pistol Pete," 43
Mason, Anthony, 53–54
Memphis State, 131
Metro Seven Conference, 130

Miami Tropics, 48–49
Micheaux, Larry, 77
Miller, Carrie, 55
Miller, Cheryl, 55, 56–57, 58, 59,
    61, 62, 64–65
Miller, Darrell, 55, 57
Miller, Reggie, 53–65
Miller, Saul, 55, 57
Miller, Saul, Sr., 56, 57, 59, 63
Mills, Richard, 70
Mind for basketball, 129
Most Valuable Player (award)
    M. Bogues, 26–27
    H. Olajuwon, 77, 80
    I. Thomas, 10, 105
    B. Williams, 113
    H. R. Williams, 128

National Basketball Association
    (NBA), 57, 64
    M. Abdul-Rauf and, 2, 8, 10
    M. Bogues and, 16, 25–27
    drug program, 48
    Eastern Conference semifinal se-
        ries, 53–54
    "hardship" rule, 104, 116
    B. Hurley and, 29, 37, 39
    J. Lucas and, 41–42, 45, 46, 47
    Most Improved Player, 12
    1994 finals, 68
    H. Olajuwon and, 79–80
    J. Starks and, 84, 86, 90–91,
        92–93
    I. Thomas and, 96, 100, 105
    B. Williams and, 109, 114,
        117–20
    H. R. Williams and, 123, 129,
        133, 134
National Basketball Association
    (NBA) All-Star Game, 93
National Basketball Association
    (NBA) draft, 44, 62, 78, 91,
    116, 132
National Basketball Association
    (NBA) finals, 68, 78, 119
NBA
    see National Basketball Associa-
        tion (NBA)
National College Athletic Associa-
    tion (NCAA), 25, 32, 78, 130

National College Athletic Associa-
    tion (NCAA) finals, 77, 124
National College Athletic Associa-
    tion (NCAA) tournament, 104
National Invitational Tournament
    (NIT) finals, 124
Nelson, Don, 91
Nestor, Ernie, 20
New Jersey Nets, 116–18, 119
New York Knicks, 53–54, 62, 80, 84,
    92–93, 120
Nigerian national basketball team,
    70, 71
North Carolina State, 24, 77
Northern Oklahoma (college), 87

Oklahoma Junior College, 87–88
Oklahoma State University, 88–91
Olajuwon, Hakeem, 67–81
Olajuwon, Kaka, 72
O'Neal, Shaquille, 80

Peplowski, Mike, 30, 34
Perfectionism
    M. Abdul-Rauf, 1–2, 3, 4, 5, 13
    J. Lucas, 43
Philadelphia 76ers, 51
Phoenix Suns, 117, 134
Physical challenges
    M. Abdul-Rauf, 2, 3, 4–5, 6, 8–9,
        10, 12
    B. Hurley, 29–39
    R. Miller, 55, 58
    H. R. Williams, 125–26
Physical size
    B. Hurley, 31, 32
    I. Thomas, 100
    see also Height; Height, lack of
Pingatore, Gene, 101
Point guard(s), 22, 85
    B. Hurley, 32
    J. Lucas, 44, 46
Point shaving, 124, 131
Pond, Christopher, 71
Portland Trail Blazers, 49, 119–20
Poverty
    J. Starks, 85–86
    I. Thomas, 96, 97–98, 103, 104
    B. Williams, 109–12, 120, 121

Practice
  M. Abdul-Rauf, 3, 8
  R. Miller, 55
  J. Starks, 89

Quad City Thunder, 92

Rebounding
  B. Williams, 109, 112–13, 115,
    117
"Redshirting," 75, 87
Reid, Robert, 76
Riley, Pat, 90, 93
Riverside (Calif.) Poly High, 58, 59
Robinson, David, 80
Rocky Mount High School, 112–13
Rodman, Dennis, 49–50, 105
Rogers State (college), 87
Role models, 9, 111
Rose, David, 72–73, 74

Sacramento Kings, 29, 30, 33–34,
    37–39
St. Amant High School, 127–28
St. Anthony High School, 30–31, 32
St. John's University, 67
St. Joseph High School, 100–102
Sampson, Ralph, 78, 115
San Antonio Spurs, 41–42, 49–50,
    91
Saulny, Kirk, 129, 130
Sawyer, Russell, 35
Scholarships, 87
  M. Abdul-Rauf, 6–7
  M. Bogues, 20
  J. Lucas, 43
  H. Olajuwon, 71
  H. R. Williams, 129
Self, Bill, 90
Slam-dunk, 84
Sonny Hill summer league, 112
Southern Mississippi, 131
Sports gambling, 130–31
Sports Illustrated, 56, 61
Starks, Irene, 85
Starks, John, 54, 83–93
Starks, Tony, 85, 86
Starks, Vincent, 86
Stockton, John, 78

Tacy, Carl, 20
Tarkanian, Jerry, 42, 49

Thomas, Alexis, 98
Thomas, Gregory, 103
Thomas, Isiah, 95–107, 120
Thomas, Larry, 100
Thomas, Mary, 95–98, 101, 102,
    103, 107
Thomas, Preston, 96
Toronto Raptors, 96
Tourette's syndrome, 2, 3, 4–5, 6,
    8–9, 10, 12
Transition game, 90
"Trash-talking," 59, 60–61
Trickey, Ken, 87–88
Tucker, Trent, 93
Tulane University, 123–24, 126,
    129–32

UCLA, 54, 56, 59–61
United States Basketball League,
    48, 132
University of Florida, 7
University of Houston (Cougars),
    67–69, 71, 72–78
University of Maryland, 43–44,
    114–16
University of North Carolina, 104,
    114
UNLV (University of Nevada at Las
    Vegas), 33

Van Nuys (Calif.) Community Hos-
    pital, 47

Wade, Bob, 15–16, 17–18, 20
Wake Forest (Demon Deacons),
    20–24
Wall, Tommy, 127–28
Walls, Kevin, 19
Walsh, Donnie, 62
Washington Bullets, 25–26
Webb, Spud, 24
Weltman, Harry, 132
Westhead, Paul, 10, 12
Whittaker, George, 92
Williams, Betty, 109–10, 111–12
Williams, Charles "Buck," 109–21
Williams, Felton, 125
Williams, John "Hot Rod," 123–34
Williams, Moses, 110
Williams, Reggie, 18
Wingate, David, 18

Wise, Skip, 16–17
Work ethic
   B. Williams, 111, 112, 115, 118,
     119
World Basketball Championships,
   24–25

World Basketball League, 92

Young, Danny, 20, 22

Zane, Jack, 43, 44